Sea Routes to Nicaragua 1851-1857

D0930784

Same inside back cover)

TROPIC OF CANCER

Gulf of Mexico

Havana

Atlantic Ocean

SHIPS FROM NEW YORK

CUBA

FLOR

ISLE OF PINES

MEXICO

DATE DUE

Caribbean Sea

BELIZE

• Belize

BAY ISLANDS   ○ ○ ← ROATAN IS.

SEPT. 12, 1860 WM. WALKER EXECUTED AT TRUXILLO BY HONDURAN FIRING SQUAD AT THE AGE OF 36

GUATEMALA

Truxillo

WILLIAM WALKER AND 58 SOLDIERS OF FORTUNE INVADED NICARAGUA, LANDING AT REALEJO JUNE 16, 1855

HONDURAS

EL SALVADOR

• Tegucigalpa

NICARAGUA

• Chinandega

León •   *Lake Managua*

Reale jo •   *Lake Nicaragua*

Managua •

Masaya •   • Bluefields

Granada •

Castillo Viejo

NICARAGUA ROUTE TO PACIFIC

San Juan del Sur

SHIPS FROM CALIFORNIA

Hacienda Santa Rosa

San José

San Juan del Norte

COSTA RICA

Gulf of Mosquitos

Aspinwall

Pacific Ocean

PANAMA

• Panama

Gulf of Panama

SCALE OF MILES

0   50   100   200

freebooters must die!

WILLIAM WALKER (1824–60)
Height 5 feet 4 inches; weight 120 pounds. Physician, lawyer, journalist, and the most notorious filibuster (soldier of fortune) of the
nineteenth century.

freebooters must die!

The life and death of William Walker,
the most notorious filibuster
of the nineteenth century

By FREDERIC ROSENGARTEN, Jr.
AUTHOR OF *The Book of Spices*

HAVERFORD HOUSE, Publishers
Wayne, Pennsylvania

F
1526.27
.W3
R67

To M. O. R.

BELIEVE IT OR NOT

BY ROBERT RIPLEY
Registered U. S. Patent Office

1942

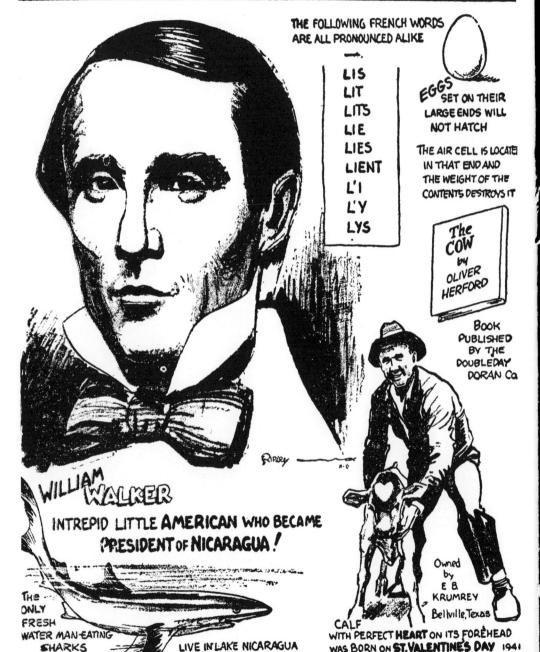

THE FOLLOWING FRENCH WORDS
ARE ALL PRONOUNCED ALIKE

LIS
LIT
LITS
LIE
LIES
LIENT
L'I
L'Y
LYS

EGGS SET ON THEIR
LARGE ENDS WILL
NOT HATCH

THE AIR CELL IS LOCATED
IN THAT END AND
THE WEIGHT OF THE
CONTENTS DESTROYS IT

The COW by OLIVER HERFORD

BOOK
PUBLISHED
BY THE
DOUBLEDAY
DORAN Co.

RIPLEY

WILLIAM WALKER
INTREPID LITTLE AMERICAN WHO BECAME
PRESIDENT OF NICARAGUA!

THE ONLY FRESH
WATER MAN-EATING
SHARKS   LIVE IN LAKE NICARAGUA

Owned by
E B KRUMREY
Bellville, Texas

CALF
WITH PERFECT **HEART** ON ITS FOREHEAD
WAS BORN ON **ST. VALENTINES DAY** 1941

FOREWORD

The author wishes to express his sincere appreciation to Dr. Alejandro Bolaños G. of Masaya, Nicaragua, for providing him with some "new" well-documented data concerning William Walker's life; likewise to Mrs. Charles P. Luckett of Louisville (William Walker's great-niece) for permission to use two nineteenth-century family portraits. Wholehearted thanks are also due to the following who have provided information or otherwise assisted him during the course of the work: Dr. Ralph Lee Woodward, Jr., chairman, Department of History, College of Arts and Sciences, Tulane University; Dr. Nancy M. Farriss, Department of History, University of Pennsylvania; Mr. Charles L. Dufour of New Orleans; Dr. David I. Folkman, Jr., of Colorado Springs; Lic. Ernesto Viteri B. of Guatemala City; Mr. Luciano Cuadra of Granada, Nicaragua; Mr. David Appel of Philadelphia; and Mr. Adolfo Midence Soto (for a photograph of Walker's grave).

The following institutions were also particularly helpful: Archivo Nacional, San José, Costa Rica; Biblioteca Nacional, San José, Costa Rica; Biblioteca Nacional y Archivo de Centro America, Guatemala City; Tennessee State Library and Archives, Nashville; The Filson Club of Louisville; Louisville Free Public Library; Latin American Library, Tulane University; Van Pelt Library, University of Pennsylvania; Library of Congress, Washington, D.C.; Huntington Library, San Marino, California; Los Angeles Public Library; British Museum Library, London; Whitney Museum of American Art, New York; The Library Company of Philadelphia; The Firestone Library, Princeton University; The Bancroft Library, University of California, Berkeley; The California Historical Society, San Francisco; and the Sutro Library, California State Library, San Francisco.

The author acknowledges his deep appreciation to Mr. Donald E. Cooke and the staff of Haverford House for their diligent cooperation during the preparation of this book; to Mrs. Kay Powell for her skillful editing; and to Mrs. Judith K. Benson for her competent collaboration in the typing of the manuscript.

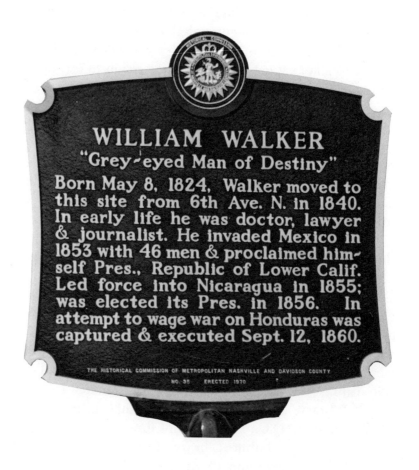

PLAQUE AT FOURTH AVENUE NORTH AND COMMERCE STREET, NASHVILLE, TENNESSEE (HOMETOWN OF WILLIAM WALKER)

INTRODUCTION

Between 1855 and 1860 William Walker's exploits in Nicaragua were almost as widely known and discussed in the United States as Watergate was over a century later. Walker was the hottest news personality between the discovery of gold in California in 1848 and the Civil War—for a time the most talked-of man in the United States. For example, on four separate dates in 1857 (February 23, March 21, March 30, and August 19), the *New-York Daily Times* devoted its entire front page to the deeds of William Walker in Nicaragua—not reporting any other news on page one. Just before the Civil War, some extremists even suggested William Walker was to the South what John Brown was to the North. Yet today probably not one U. S. citizen in ten thousand has ever heard of William Walker—a lost character in American history.

But although forgotten even in his home state of Tennessee, William Walker is still vividly remembered in Central America, with some justification, as a devil with horns and a tail. Elementary school textbooks proudly acclaim the Filibuster War of 1855–57, in which the ruthless imperialistic invader William Walker and his Yankee mercenaries were driven out of Nicaragua by the combined heroic forces of the five Central American republics. United States history texts, on the other hand, rarely mention Walker's name and his venture in Nicaragua, perhaps preferring to sweep this ignominious episode of flagrant Yankee imperialism under the rug.

The name William Walker suggests neither stirring adventure nor bold undertaking. Nevertheless, Walker was the "king of the filibusters" in the middle of the nineteenth century; with a reckless little band of fifty-eight men he invaded Nicaragua in 1855 and a year later became president of that country. In those days the term filibuster usually meant a soldier of fortune, especially a freebooter, adventurer, or "land pirate" who participated in a revolution in a foreign country in order to enrich himself.

The zealous Walker was interested in power rather than riches. But it was not in power for power's sake: he felt he had a mission and that power was needed to complete his mission, which, for better or for worse, was to "regenerate" Central America. Had he accomplished what he had in mind, he would have (1) made a slave empire out of Central America, with himself as dictator; and (2) built through Nicaragua the canal that was to be constructed in Panama some sixty years later.

In doing so this Yankee imperialist would have destroyed the Spanish-American cultural heritage of Nicaragua and the other Central American countries and replaced it with a ruthless Anglo-Saxon autocracy. The renowned Nicaraguan poet Rubén Darío (1867–1916), who became a revolutionary force in Spanish verse, calls our attention to this threat in *Los Cisnes;* referring to gringo intervention in Central America, he asks:

> "Seremos entregados a los bárbaros fieros?
> Tantos millones de hombres hablaremos inglés?
> Ya no hay nobles hidalgos ni bravos caballeros?
> Callaremos ahora para llorar después?"

> (Will we be handed over to the barbarian hordes?
> Will millions of us have to speak English?
> Are there no more noble hidalgos or courageous knights?
> Will we be quiet now, only to weep later?)

Walker did not live to see his dreams realized. Instead, he was shot by a firing squad in Truxillo, Honduras, in September 1860 at the age of thirty-six.

This is the story of William Walker, the "gray-eyed man of destiny," the last and greatest filibuster. Walker's unusual, controversial life is presented essentially in narrative form, without moral judgments. It was not just William Walker's eyes that were gray—so was his life: neither black nor white, neither all bad nor all good.

CONTENTS

WALKER AS A YOUTH
The earliest-known portrait of William Walker. Nashville, circa 1841.

1

Gentle Youth

WILLIAM WALKER'S quiet boyhood gave no clue to his dramatic future. He was born in Nashville, Tennessee, on May 8, 1824, the eldest of four children. His father was a Scot named James Walker who had settled in Nashville in 1820 to enter the mercantile and insurance business; his mother was Mary Norvell from Kentucky. William had two brothers, Norvell and James, and a sister, Alice.

As a youth he was so quiet and refined that he was sometimes considered a mama's boy and a sissy. Since his mother was a consumptive invalid, young Walker spent many hours reading aloud to her. At school he was bright, well behaved, and unusually precocious: in 1838 he graduated from the University of Nashville at the age of fourteen. Years later a woman friend of his mother's observed that young William was "very intelligent and as refined in his feeling as a girl. I used often to go to see his mother and always found him entertaining her in some way."

At sixteen he obtained a second degree from Nashville, equivalent to an M.A., with special emphasis on study of the Bible as well as Latin and Greek classics; his other courses included English composition, geometry, trigonometry, ancient history and geography, mineralogy, logic, philosophy, political economy, navigation, international law, and oratory. He was president of his college debating society. For a youth of his time Walker enjoyed exceptional educational advantages and made the most of them.

ALICE WALKER
William's younger sister, who in
1854 married Lawrence Richardson
of Lexington, Kentucky, and became
the mother of eleven children.

His early home environment was puritanically austere, with much emphasis on prayer, Bible study, church attendance, morality, and chastity. Frivolous pastimes were forbidden, and there were no organized sports. William grew up in an atmosphere of all work and no play—a monastic life with very strict discipline. His parents wanted him to enter the Protestant ministry (Christian Disciples' Church), but although he was primarily interested in politics, he decided to study medicine. After eighteen months of training at the medical department of the University of Pennsylvania, he received the degree of Doctor of Medicine in March 1843. The subject of his final medical essay was "The Structure and Function of the Iris."

During the next two years he lived in Europe. Six months of continued study of medicine in Paris convinced him that he did not want to be a physician. He traveled for another year and a half through France, England, Germany, and Italy—observing, philosophizing, and making vague plans for the future. Withdrawn and austere, he made few European friends. He disliked the French and was repelled by the gay night life and licentious ladies of Paris.

Walker was, in fact, a young, idealistic Puritan. The external gaiety and ruthless cynicism of the French disgusted him. He didn't drink, smoke, or gamble, avoided brothels, and resisted Gallic temptations; his main pleasure seems to have been reading the works of Victor Hugo.

While in Europe, he carried on an active correspondence with John Berrien Lindsley, a boyhood friend and former classmate at the University of Nashville, who subsequently became a distinguished physician and founder of the medical school at that university. Although Walker never married, he wrote some sound, mature suggestions to Lindsley in November 1844:

> I hope you have given up your idea of becoming a missionary, and purpose taking up your abode in some civilized part of the world where a fellow can have a chance of seeing you now and then. Ah! John, it is a hard thing to live in the world without our natural friends —those whom birth has given us. So, I hope you have fallen, or will fall, in love with some young lady near Nashville and get married; and I hope like a true *cara sposa*, she will govern you completely and not let you emigrate into any outlandish region where you will have no companions but gibbering savages or half-civilized pagans.

UNIVERSITY OF PENNSYLVANIA, PHILADELPHIA
William Walker was a medical student at Medical Hall (left foreground), near Ninth and Chestnut streets, from 1841 to 1843.

*Candidates for the Degree
of Doctor of Medicine
in the University of Pennsylvania
W. E. Horner M. D.
Dean*

Candidates 1843.

Class	N°	Name	State	Ad Exam. Address	Essay	Prof.	Result	Credit
4th	xii 1	William Walker	Ten:	18 5 8"	Struct. & Funct. of Iris	Hr 25th	Passed	By cash $40.
	v 2	Edw. M. Parham	Va	21 Jansom.	Leucorrhea	Norge 21	Passed	By cash $40.
	vi 3	Flavius Aug. Byrd	Ala.	37 4th 10"	In Hom° of Eye	Se 26th	Passed	By cash $40.
	vi 4	Thomas W. Mason	Ala.	37 4th 10"	Acute Arthritis	Ch 25	Passed	By cash $40.
	v 5	Ralph Butterfield	Mass	14 Jansom	Intermit. Fever	Jn 21	Passed	By cash $40.
	v 6	William L. A. Richards	Del.	14 Jansom	In Febr. Biliosi Remit.	W 21	Passed	By cash $40.

ON MARCH 31, 1843, WILLIAM WALKER WAS ONE OF 114 CANDI-
DATES WHO RECEIVED AN M.D. DEGREE AT THE UNIVERSITY OF
PENNSYLVANIA; HIS ESSAY WAS ON "THE STRUCTURE AND FUNC-
TION OF THE IRIS"

Instead of following the conservative advice he gave Lindsley,
Walker eventually did exactly the opposite.

Another letter from Walker to Lindsley, written from Paris
during the same period, shows the sensitive and facile writing
style of the future soldier of fortune. One wonders how the
individual who formulated these thoughtful, perceptive lines
could, within ten years, become so deeply involved in aggressive, predatory bloodshed; yet there is a vague foreboding of
future disaster in this portrayal of early impressions:

You speak of your early impressions; early impressions are hard to
erase. They are like the figures which we make on caoutchouc; by
an exertion of force you may stretch the *gum elastic* until the figures
disappear; but when you relax your efforts, they resume their original
character. It is said that no idea which enters our mind is ever entirely
removed; often, we see the spectre, as it were, of our departed notions
or opinions. By experience, I know how firm is the hold of these early
and long-cherished ideas. With me, whilst a child and a boy, I had
determined on a political career; there have been times when I thought
that the last .vestige of such an idea had disappeared, but often it re-
appears to me, in my waking dreams, leaving me uncertain whether
it be an angel of light or an angel of darkness.

In 1845 Walker returned to Nashville and began to study law; he completed his legal training in New Orleans and was admitted to the bar of Louisiana, a state that still followed the Napoleonic Code. He soon became restless and dissatisfied as a lawyer and, taking advantage of his special talent for writing, turned to journalism.

In 1848 Walker became an editor of the New Orleans *Daily Crescent*, a controversial newspaper that Southerners considered to be pro-Yankee, antislavery, and extremely liberal in its views. Its editorials even advocated women's rights to suffrage and property, thus incurring the ridicule of the chauvinistic male population of New Orleans.

Proslavery jingoists in the South wanted to annex Cuba to the United States. Its proximity to Florida and New Orleans, fertile soil, favorable climate, and successful exploitation of slave labor made the "Pearl of the Antilles" a desirable prize. The island's wealth and resources could be used to counteract Northern power. This popular Southern viewpoint was vividly expressed by J. D. B. De Bow in *De Bow's Review:*

> The North Americans will spread out far beyond their present bounds. They will encroach again and again on their neighbors. New territories will be planted, declare their independence and be annexed. We have New Mexico and California! We will have Old Mexico and Cuba!

Ardent expansionists were secretly planning and financing a filibustering invasion of Cuba under the leadership of General Narciso López, which was supposed to drive out the Spanish, form a new proslavery revolutionary government, and then apply for annexation of the island to the American Union. After annexation, Cuba could be carved into two slave states, augmenting the South's political power in the Union. This clandestine expedition by López (which was to fail disastrously in the summer of 1849) was exposed and condemned in *Crescent* editorials, some of which were written by William Walker. While the *Crescent* favored the annexation of Cuba to the United States, it advocated compromise and conciliation with Spain, not aggressive military tactics; furthermore, it was unsympathetic to the Southern desire for expansion in order to promote slavery.

Needless to say, the *Crescent*'s conciliatory editorials were often viewed unfavorably in the South. At the time Walker stood quite far to the left, but today his progressive thoughts seem contradictory, for within a few years he was to practice most violently precisely what he had preached against.

In October 1848 Walker was invited to Nashville to deliver the commencement address at his alma mater. In a lengthy speech—"The Unity of Art"—that must have seemed interminable to some restless students, Walker acknowledged that he was deeply moved by heroism in the arts, by heroic poetry and heroic action as exemplified by Byron. Although he died young, Byron was old in fame and deeds because he had lived artistically yet heroically. Heroic behavior was an important form of aesthetic art to Walker, perhaps more vital than conventional common sense; in fact, he went on, man's artistic talent can even be expressed through courageous action in a patriotic war. This address exalting heroism, given when Walker was twenty-four, foreshadowed future daring adventures in his own life.

THE DAILY CRESCENT.

By A. H. HAYES & CO.

A. H. HAYES..J. C. LARUE..S. F. WILSON, WM. WALKER.

Office -- No. 95 St. Charles Street.

TERMS OF THE CRESCENT.

DAILY—*Fifteen Cents a Week*, payable to the carriers, weekly.... or, *Eight Dollars* per year—half yearly and quarterly at the same rates—in advance.....Single copies, *Five Cents*.........
The office will receipt for all subscriptions exceeding one week

THE WEEKLY CRESCENT will be furnished to single subscribers at THREE DOLLARS per year; to clubs of four or more, directed to the same Post-office, at Two Dollars and Fifty Cents a year each; Postmasters and others who may act as Agents, and send orders, paid, for ten copies, will receive one copy in addition for their compensation. *Payable in all cases in advance.* Single papers or packages, in wrappers, can be had at the office of publication, No. 95 St. Charles street.

ADVERTISEMENTS—not exceeding twelve lines, in Agate type, $' for the first insertion, and 50 cents for every subsequent insertion. Those of greater length in proportion. Notices on the second page, of ten lines in Pearl type, $1 each insertion.

Advertisements published weekly, semi-weekly, tri-weekly or monthly, are charged $1 per square for every insertion. A liberal discount made to those who advertise by the year.

NEW ORLEANS:

THURSDAY MORNING, JUNE 21, 1849.

BETWEEN 1848 AND EARLY 1850 WILLIAM WALKER WAS ONE OF THE EDITORS AND OWNERS OF THE "DAILY CRESCENT" IN NEW ORLEANS

2

Tragedy in New Orleans

I N NEW ORLEANS, Walker met a young Virginia lawyer and man-about-town named Edmund Randolph, a grandson
of George Washington's attorney general of the same name
Randolph, five years older than Walker, exerted considerable
influence on the latter in his emphasis on Anglo-Saxon tradition;
they discussed world history and grandiose, idealistic plans for
the future.

Randolph introduced Walker to the only love of his life, a
charming New Orleans brunette a year younger than himself
named Ellen Galt Martin. The twenty-three-year-old Ellen was
desirable, beautiful, intelligent—and a deaf mute. As they fell
deeply in silent love, Walker added the sign language to his
other intellectual accomplishments.

Ellen's family was well-to-do. Walker frequently called at
the Martin home on Julia Street, in the aristocratic section of
New Orleans known as "the Thirteen Houses." Despite her
physical handicaps, Ellen was vivacious, attractive, and popular. She enjoyed dances and parties and other gay New Orleans
social events, charming her friends into forgetting that she
could neither speak nor hear.

Walker, on the other hand, cannot have been a very impres-
sive-looking lover. He was five feet four inches tall, very thin,
and weighed about 120 pounds. His hands were small and
delicate. His hair was light brown, his jaw angular. He seldom
smiled and never laughed. His most impressive features were

7

WILLIAM WALKER'S FIANCÉE

Ellen Galt Martin (a deaf mute) in fancy-dress costume. Her tragic death in 1849 apparently caused a violent change in Walker's personality.

his gray eyes, which were brilliant and penetrating—almost hypnotic. His shy and soft-spoken ways during the period when he was courting Ellen gave no indication of Walker's latent aggressive power.

Despite his looks and shyness, the taciturn Walker managed to court Ellen with success. A date was set for the wedding that was never to take place.

Yellow fever and cholera were perennial plagues in New Orleans. Yellow fever usually struck in the hot summer months, but cholera could annihilate its victims at any time. Early in 1849 scores of death notices were already being published, as a rampant cholera epidemic swept through the gloomy city. Businesses virtually came to a halt, stores and theaters were closed, EPIDEMIC signs were widespread. Countless processions of hearses passed row upon row of closely shuttered houses. Suddenly, to Walker's intense grief and anguish, his beloved Ellen died of cholera; her death notice appeared in the New Orleans newspapers on April 19, 1849:

DIED

On Wednesday April 18, at half-past 1 P. M., ELLEN GALT (MARTIN) daughter of the late Mr. John Martin. The friends and acquaintances of the family are invited to attend her funeral THIS AFTERNOON at half past 4 o'clock, from 131 Julia Street.

Before Ellen's death Walker was described by those who knew him as quiet, serious, gentle, and kind. Now his entire personality changed, as Dr. Jekyll was transformed into Mr. Hyde. Walker became melancholy, occasionally almost paranoid in his behavior, and obsessed with a longing for reckless and daring action regardless of the consequences, presumably to bring solace for his deep sorrow.

3

Manifest Destiny and Filibustering:
Narciso López and
William L. Crittenden
Executed in Cuba

As AN EDITOR of the *Crescent*, Walker came into constant contact with one of the most popular causes of the times: Manifest Destiny (sometimes called the Spread Eagle Doctrine), which he came to believe in ardently and on which he was to base his subsequent career. The term Manifest Destiny first appeared in July 1845, in an article in the *United States Magazine and Democratic Review* by John L. O'Sullivan, who championed the divine right of the American people "to overspread the continent." Representative Robert C. Winthrop of Massachusetts repeated the phrase later that same year on the floor of the House of Representatives, when he argued during the debate about Oregon that it was "our manifest destiny to spread over the whole continent."

In the mid-nineteenth century Manifest Destiny meant territorial expansion into ill-defined areas in North America and the Western Hemisphere. This virile philosophy held great appeal for the American public, who fervently believed that the rapid expansion of the past decades should continue. There was no reason why the growth of the United States should stop with the annexation of Texas in 1845 and the acquisition of California in 1848, at the end of the Mexican War. Further expansion was justified—either northward to Canada or southward to Mexico, Cuba, and Central America.

The 1850s were the heyday of aggressive expansionism. Franklin Pierce was the first American president to declare—

in his inaugural address in 1853—that territorial aggrandizement was an objective of his incoming administration. James Buchanan, his successor, prophesied that "expansion is in the future the policy of our country, and only cowards fear and oppose it."

"Backward" territories, where rich natural resources were being misused, should be taken over, and all that had to be given in exchange was the prospect of admission to the Union. It was America's mission continually to go ahead and every few years swallow up, with unbridled passion and enthusiasm, still more territory—either by purchase, annexation, military conquest, or almost any other convenient means.

A belligerent poet in John L. O'Sullivan's *Democratic Review* summed up a growing, vigorous America's right to more space:

> We can not help the matter if we would;
> The race must have expansion—we must grow
> Though every forward footstep be withstood
> And every inch of ground presents its foe.

The phenomenon of filibustering, which flourished between 1840 and 1860, was a natural outgrowth of Manifest Destiny. Filibusters or freebooters (from the Dutch *vrijbuiter*, meaning plunderer) were soldiers of fortune who engaged in fitting out expeditions to and conducting unauthorized warfare against countries with which the United States was at peace—usually with the aim of enriching themselves. The term was first applied to buccaneers in the West Indies who preyed on the Spanish commerce to South America; later it was used to describe adventurers such as the ones who followed López to Cuba and Walker to Nicaragua in their expeditions of conquest. Today the word filibuster, considerably tamed, has an entirely different meaning and refers to the tactics used by a minority group of a legislative body, usually the Senate, to obstruct the passage of a bill: long-winded speeches, introduction of irrelevant issues, and so on. In other words, filibustering today means talking a bill to death, while in the 1850s it meant "saying it with bullets."

Expansionists, although most vociferous in the South, were

also to be found in the North and West. Many white North Americans considered themselves superior to the generally darker mixed races inhabiting Mexico, Central America, and the Caribbean. Haughty, self-righteous Americans belittled their neighbors south of the border, characterizing them as barbarous, ignorant "greasers" who needed to be regenerated. It was the duty of the United States, proclaimed these bigoted expansionists, to annex and "uplift" the miserable, backward, unenlightened peoples, who had demonstrated themselves to be totally incapable and unworthy of self-rule. Of course the economic benefits that would accrue to the United States from grabbing the fertile soils and magnificent natural resources of the tropics of the Western Hemisphere were not just incidental.

In *The War in Nicaragua* William Walker was later to justify his own militant actions south of the border in lucid terms quite unacceptable by today's standards, but applauded by many in the 1850s as a natural and desirable expression of rugged imperialism:

> That which you ignorantly call "Filibusterism" is not the offspring of hasty passion or ill-regulated desire; it is the fruit of the sure, unerring instincts which act in accordance with laws as old as creation. They are but drivellers who speak of establishing fixed relations between the pure white American race, as it exists in the United States, and the mixed Hispano-Indian race, as it exists in Mexico and Central America, without the employment of force. The history of the world presents no such Utopian vision as that of an inferior race yielding meekly and peacefully to the controlling influence of a superior people.

Before 1850 expansionists of both North and South were in favor of the acquisition of new United States territories, but as the Civil War approached, Manifest Destiny gradually became more sectionalized. Northern expansionists believed that young America had a mission: to spread the ideals of democracy and freedom, a goal that could best be realized by enlarging the country. The Southern expansionists, who were the more zealous, saw a chance to extend slavery. Ardent promoters of slavery claimed that whenever this institution was confined within certain specified territorial limits, its future was doomed —owing to the rapid exhaustion of the soil, the overplanting of crops such as cotton and sugarcane, and the rapid natural increase of the slave population. For the comfort and happiness of the slaves and the benefit of the landowners, therefore, slavery required fresh lands, plenty of virgin forests, and water. Furthermore, political leaders in the South believed that new slave territory was needed to maintain an equilibrium between slave and free states; what better way than to extend slavery into Mexico, Cuba, and Central America?

Cuba was a naturally tempting target for expansion, being only ninety miles away, and the United States tried to purchase the island from Spain for $100 million in 1848—unsuccessfully. This diplomatic failure led to the emergence of a dynamic if ineffectual revolutionist who was constantly in the public eye: General Narciso López.

López had been born in Venezuela in 1798, the son of a wealthy merchant. As a youth he served as a commissioned officer in the Spanish army in Venezuela. Handsome, imposing in physique, an accomplished horseman with an affable personality, he was a favorite with his troops. López moved to Spain, where he pursued his military career, rising to the rank of general. After a few years he retired from the Spanish army and was appointed to a lucrative political post on the island of Cuba. Besides his political activities he also became involved in several business enterprises there, principally copper mines and coffee plantations, which failed for various reasons. He suffered large gambling losses, incurred substantial debts, and fell out of favor politically.

Embittered by his loss of wealth and influence, he intrigued against the Spanish government and took part in a clandestine revolutionary plot in 1848: a secret insurrection to free Cuba from Spanish rule. When this conspiracy was discovered by the local authorities, López had to flee for his life to the United States. In Cuba he was condemned to death in absentia. In New York, López found that an active movement for the forcible annexation of Cuba to the United States was under way. A filibustering expedition was being organized that was to consist of some five thousand men and be financed by $3 million.

Some financial aid was obtained from Cuban exiles, New York friends, and certain wealthy Southerners. When both Jefferson Davis and Robert E. Lee turned down the leadership of the expedition, the charismatic López became its natural leader. But this abortive filibustering movement against Cuba was stopped by federal authorities in September 1849 at Round Island, near New Orleans.

Undaunted, López continued to gather recruits, mostly from Ohio, Kentucky, Mississippi, and Louisiana. Many Americans, especially in the South and West, sympathized with him. His financial support, which was less than originally hoped for, came for the most part from wealthy New Orleans extremists, whose avowed aim was to free Cuba from Spain, temporarily establish an independent Cuban republic, and then eventually annex Cuba to the American Union as a slave state.

In May 1850 López's first formal attempt to invade Cuba was launched from the island of Contoy, near Yucatán, although it had originated in New Orleans. This was called the Cárdenas Expedition because the initial landing of about 520 "Liberators" from the steamer *Creole* was made at Cárdenas, a town on the Bay of Cárdenas, about ninety miles east of Havana.

Early on the morning of May 19 the *Creole* crept silently into the Bay of Cárdenas but had not proceeded very far when she ran aground and became firmly stuck on a coral reef. A brave young filibuster named Callender I. Fayssoux (who was later to serve with William Walker in Nicaragua) immediately distinguished himself by swimming off to the shore with a rope between his teeth, thus pulling the ship off the reef and enabling his companions to land.

Cárdenas was known as the "American City," since so many Americans were engaged in business there that English was widely spoken. It was anticipated that the local population would support López with enthusiasm and join him in the liberation struggle against the bloody tyranny of Spain. Such was the case during the first morning of the invasion, when many native Cubans cheered the invading force of red-shirted Liberators—and some even joined the Americans. On the second

NARCISO LÓPEZ
Venezuelan-born filibuster who identified himself with revolutionaries in Cuba. López organized several unsuccessful filibustering expeditions from the United States to Cuba. He was captured in 1851 and executed by the Spanish in Havana—strangled by the garrote before a howling mob of twenty thousand spectators.

day, however, the regular Spanish army of 700 well-trained soldiers attacked the invaders. Most of the local Cubans then hurriedly took off their red shirts and joined their Spanish masters; the Cuban patriots who had fought with the Liberators of López in the morning changed their minds as well as their shirts in the afternoon, taking up arms with the Spanish regulars and demonstrating their loyalty to Spain.

Despite this perfidy, the invading troops managed to drive the Spaniards out of Cárdenas. General López decided to re-embark his liberating army on the *Creole* and move to another point on the coast, where he had loyal personal friends. Unfortunately, while leaving the Bay of Cárdenas the *Creole* ran aground again on another sunken coral reef. The entire supply of arms, munitions, and provisions had to be dumped overboard to enable the vessel to glide off the bar. López still wanted to proceed with the invasion, even without arms and supplies, but the men protested that such a plan would be suicidal. López was overruled, and the *Creole,* although somewhat damaged, headed for Key West, Florida, as rapidly as its defective steam power would permit.

Early on the morning of May 21, when the *Creole* was within forty miles of Key West, the fast and armipotent steamer *Pizarro* was observed in the distance; she was rapidly gaining on the limping *Creole.* In a dramatic race the Cuban Liberators managed to gain the sanctuary of Key West harbor just ahead of the *Pizarro.* Thus ended the Cárdenas Expedition. The *Creole* was confiscated by the United States authorities, but no filibusters were apprehended. López was arrested later in Savannah but released for lack of evidence.

The Cuban revolutionist was a popular hero in the South but a source of constant vexation and embarrassment to the vacillating administration in Washington, which was in a quandary about how to deal with filibusters. The American government was stung by foreign criticism: England and especially Spain wanted the filibusters to be severely punished as pirates; public opinion on the other hand was so strongly on the side of López and his followers that a conviction for violating the nebulous

Neutrality Law of 1818 (which forbade organizing within the United States an armed force that intended to attack a friendly foreign power) would be imprudent.

Having escaped with his life, López lost no time in organizing a second invasion of Cuba. He sent agents to stir up trouble in various parts of the island and incite the Creoles to open revolt against the Spanish. Although he could not speak English, López managed to attract many volunteers in the United States with the slogan "López and Liberty"—not only lovers of liberty for liberty's sake and lovers of adventure for adventure's sake, but also volunteers who expected to collect a bounty of four thousand dollars, or its equivalent in Cuban real estate, if the invasion succeeded.

Many valiant and idealistic young men from the South were eager for the fray. Among them was Colonel William Logan Crittenden, tall and handsome, a born soldier, the scion of a distinguished Kentucky family. (His uncle, John J. Crittenden,

COLONEL WILLIAM L. CRITTENDEN
A graduate of West Point, he was executed by a firing squad in Havana during Narciso López's disastrous filibustering expedition of 1851.

was attorney general of the United States.) W. L. Crittenden was a graduate of West Point who had served with distinction and conspicuous gallantry in the Mexican War, but he resigned from the United States Army to cast his lot with Narciso López.

The second López invasion of Cuba, known as the Bahía Honda Expedition, might more aptly have been described as a chain of horrors. It started on a happy note: the transport steamer *Pampero* was enthusiastically cheered by a New Orleans crowd as she sailed from the Lafayette Street pier early on the morning of August 3, 1851. Some caution had to be observed to avoid seizure by federal authorities. Luckily, the 434 adventurers, mostly Anglo-Saxon in origin, were unaware of the incredible tragedy that awaited them as they sailed lightheartedly toward Cuba on the calm, blue waters of the Gulf of Mexico under a pleasant tropical sun. After an uneventful voyage the *Pampero* landed at daybreak on August 12 near Bahía Honda on the Cuban coast, some seventy miles west of Havana. The disastrous military effort that ensued was similar in many respects to the abortive Bay of Pigs fiasco by Cuban exiles 110 years later. In both instances the popular uprisings of patriotic Cubans that were supposed to take place—in 1851 against Spanish rule and in 1961 against Fidel Castro—never materialized.

On the contrary, when the Liberators of López landed at Morillo, near Bahía Honda, instead of being welcomed by enthusiastic Creole friends offering them supplies and horses, they were greeted by a volley of hostile and deadly Creole musketry. The native Cuban population was not yet ready to be freed from the dominion of Spain. López's badly organized and vastly outnumbered invading troops were soon surrounded and attacked on all sides by well-prepared Spanish regulars. The Spanish had been informed of López's every movement by his so-called Creole friends.

Colonel Crittenden, with 130 men, was soon cut off from General López and the main body of the expeditionary force. The Kentucky colonel had been ordered to protect the arms, ammunition, and supplies of the Liberators until transport wagons could be obtained and sent to him by López. The wagons never came. Fighting valiantly against superior odds, Crittenden and his detachment attempted to join López; the supplies were loaded onto ox carts which bogged down on the muddy roads. After marching all night Crittenden's group was overwhelmed by Spanish troops. Crittenden ordered and led a charge, a diversionary tactic to enable a detachment of 80 men under Captain J. A. Kelly to proceed toward López with the ox carts. Kelly succeeded in joining López, but in the meantime had been forced to abandon the arms and supplies.

Crittenden and his 50 remaining invaders were soon overwhelmed by several hundred Spanish troops. Fighting gallantly, the Americans attempted to cut through the dense chaparral and heavy forest to look for López. But López had retreated to the mountains. Finding their situation utterly hopeless, Crittenden and his group managed to reach the coastal village of Morillo, where they put to sea in four fishing boats. They were soon sighted by the heavily armed Spanish steamer *Habanero,* whose artillery forced them to surrender. Under the terms agreed upon, Crittenden and his men would be treated in all respects as prisoners of war and their lives would be spared.

But the captain general of Cuba, José de la Concha, utterly disregarded the terms of surrender: he ordered the captives to be tried by a drumhead court-martial and executed immediately. A proclamation was issued ordering the execution by a firing squad of Colonel Crittenden and his comrades—fifty-one men in all. Since the group consisted mostly of Americans (there were forty Americans, four Irishmen, two Cubans, two Hungarians, one Scot, one Italian, and one native of the Philippine Islands), the wretched prisoners asked to see the American consul. Their request was denied. Instead, they were given half an hour to write personal letters of farewell to their families and friends.

Just before he was executed in Havana, twenty-eight-year-old Colonel William Logan Crittenden wrote the following tragic letter, which may give some insight into the thinking of filibuster leaders—who must have known that sooner or later a violent and unpleasant end almost certainly awaited them. The letter, dated August 16, 1851, was written aboard the Spanish warship *Esperanza,* where the captives were confined, and addressed to a friend in the United States, Dr. Lucien Hensley:

Dear Lucien:

In half an hour I, with fifty others, am to be shot. We were taken prisoners yesterday. We were in small boats. General López separated the balance of the command from me. I had with me about one hundred—was attacked by two battalions of infantry and one company of horse. The odds were too great, and strange to tell I was not furnished with a single musket cartridge. López did not get any artillery. I have not the heart to write to any of my family. If the truth ever comes out you will find that I did my duty, and have the perfect confidence of every man with me. We had retired from the field and were going to sea, and were overtaken by the Spanish steamer *Habanero,* and captured. Tell General Houston that his nephew got separated from me on the 13th, the day of the fight and I have not seen him since. He may have straggled off and joined López, who advanced rapidly to the interior. My people, however, were entirely surrounded on every side. We saw that we have been deceived grossly, and were making for the United States, when taken. During my short sojourn on this island I have not met a single patriot. We landed some forty or fifty miles to the westward of this, and I am sure that in that part of the island López has no friends. When I was attacked López was only three miles off. If he had not been deceiving us as to the state of things, he would have fallen back with his force and made fight, instead of which he marched on immediately to the interior. I am requested to get you to tell Mr. Green of the custom house that his brother shares my fate. Victor Ker is also with me, also Standford. I recollect no others of your acquaintance at present. I will die like a man. My heart has not failed me yet, nor do I believe it will. Communicate with my family. . . .

This is an incoherent letter, but the circumstances must excuse me. My hands are swollen to double their thickness, resulting from having been too tightly corded for the last eighteen hours. Write to Whistlar and let him write to my mother. I am afraid the news will break her heart. My heart beats warmly toward her now.

Farewell. My love to all my friends. I am sorry that I die owing a cent, but it is inevitable.

Yours, Strong in Heart,
W. L. Crittenden

This letter was stained with blood from Crittenden's lacerated wrists.

Another moving farewell was written at the same time, under the same lamentable conditions, by Captain Victor Ker to his wife:

My dear Felicia:

Adieu, my dear wife. This is the last letter you will receive from your Victor. In one hour I shall be no more. Embrace all of my friends for me. Never marry again; it is my desire. My adieu to my sisters and brothers. Again, a last adieu. I die like a soldier.

August 16, 6 o'clock, 1851

Your husband,
Victor

The prisoners were marched down the gangway of the *Esperanza* in single file, with their hands tied behind their backs, into a ferryboat that transported them to the place of execution. Some twelve hundred troops had gathered on the slopes of a hill near Castle Atares, about three-quarters of a mile outside Havana (the rest of the army had been sent out in pursuit of General López). The Spanish soldiers, attired in battle dress but wearing straw hats, formed a square; in the background several thousand citizens of Havana had come out to watch the gory massacre, as they would a bullfight. The mayor of Havana read the death sentence, and the tragedy commenced.

The victims, securely bound and blindfolded, were led forward six at a time and commanded to kneel with their backs to the soldiers who were to shoot them. After each group of six was murdered, the corpses were pushed aside to make room for the next lot. A lad of fifteen begged in vain to speak to someone who knew English. Those who were not killed instantly were beaten to death.

Colonel Crittenden, as the commanding officer of the party, was shot first of all, and alone. He refused to kneel, did not allow himself to be blindfolded, and would not turn his back to the firing squad. His last words were: "A Kentuckian kneels to none except his God, and always dies facing his enemy." Standing erect, looking the death-dealing muskets in the muzzle, he bravely met his doom.

The bodies were then handed over to the bloodthirsty mob, who spat on them, kicked them, mutilated them, and stripped them of their clothing. The naked, bloody corpses were then piled onto old hearses and carted ignominiously to the heretic section of the Espada cemetery, dumped into a common trench, and covered with quicklime.

In contrast to the heroic tragedy of W. L. Crittenden is the story of a fifty-second filibuster: David Q. Rousseau, also of Kentucky, who is reputed to have gained his eventual freedom in an ingenious manner. Cast into jail with the other fifty-one prisoners, he was informed that he was going to be shot on the following day. As a kindly gesture, he, like Crittenden and Ker, was granted permission by his captors to write one letter to inform a friend or relative of his approaching execution. Apparently Rousseau had no relatives and few friends. Indeed, he felt ashamed—the other prisoners around him were hurriedly writing their last letters, and he hadn't even started his own. To whom should he write? Then a brilliant thought occurred to him: all the letters would probably be opened by the Spanish censors, so why not pick a really important "friend"—say, Daniel Webster, the secretary of state in Washington (even though he didn't even know Webster). So he composed the following note:

> Dan, my dear old boy, how little you thought when we parted at the close of that last agreeable visit of a week, which I paid you the other day, that within a month I should be "cribbed, cabined, and confined" in the infernal hole of a dungeon from which I indite this. I wish you would send the Spanish minister a case of that very old Madeira of yours, which he professes to prefer to the wines of his own country, and tell him the silly scrape I have got myself into, if indeed it be not too late, for they talk of sending me to "the bourne" tomorrow. However, one never can believe a word these rascals say, so I write this in the hope that they are lying as usual,—and am, my dear old schoolmate, your affectionate friend,
>
> Dave

Rousseau's lack of friends turned out to be a blessing. He was rewarded for his clear thinking under stress, for while all the other filibusters in his group were executed by the Spanish, apparently he alone was spared. He was condemned instead to two years' hard labor in chains in the quicksilver mines in Ceuta in Spanish Morocco, a sentence later commuted to eighteen months. Surviving that ordeal, he lived to serve through the Civil War as a lieutenant in the Kentucky Infantry of the Union army.

While Crittenden and his followers were being captured and executed, General Narciso López was beset by problems of his own. With an inadequately supplied force of four hundred Liberators, including Captain Kelly's detachment, he vainly struggled against a far greater number of Spanish troops. López lost some forty-four men, including killed and wounded, in the battle of Las Pozas, and then retreated to a coffee plantation called Cafetal de Frias, which had previously belonged to him but had been confiscated three years earlier. Here he made a stand and, although attacked by nine hundred of the enemy, won a decisive battle, forcing the Spanish troops to retreat.

Having waited in vain for some three thousand reinforcements from New Orleans that never arrived, López decided to withdraw his own men to the mountains nearby. Unfortunately, a very severe tropical rainstorm virtually ruined the Liberators' weapons and their entire remaining supply of ammunition. Heading toward Bahia Honda in a vain effort to find some Creole patriots who would rally to their support, López and his followers were attacked once more by a large contingent of fresh enemy troops. The badly organized, exhausted Liberators, without ammunition, lacking provisions, and having had but one meal in six days, were routed and many were killed and wounded. General López himself made a futile effort to escape but was tracked down and severely bitten by bloodhounds and then captured by seventeen hostile Creoles on August 29, just seventeen days after his landing. The Creoles, many of them small farmers, almost without exception adhered to the royal Spanish cause and violently opposed López and the Liberators.

At seven o'clock on the morning of September 2, weary and wounded, Narciso López was strangled by the garrote in a public square near the Carcel in Havana, before a howling mob of some twenty thousand spectators. Dressed in a long white garment resembling a shroud, with a hood over his head and a priest on either side, López slowly followed an escort of uniformed guards and priests with long black caps, carrying a black banner. The ominous procession crossed the square and halted at the base of the scaffold.

The Negro executioner, two priests, two officers, and the unfortunate López climbed up on a platform about twenty feet high where the garrote had already been set up. It consisted of a small upright post to which an iron collar was attached in front, and at the back of which was a large iron screw. The priests recited a long prayer while López knelt before them. After repeatedly kissing a crucifix López uttered his last words in a firm voice: "My countrymen, pardon me for the evil, if any, that I may have caused you. I have not intended any evil—only good. I die for my beloved Cuba. Farewell."

López sat down on a stool attached to the garrote. The executioner adjusted the collar around his neck, gave two powerful turns of the screw, and thus ended the life of the patriot Narciso López.

His remaining followers, 173 in number, were subsequently embarked for the Spanish penal colony at Ceuta to serve long sentences at hard labor in the quicksilver mines. Queen Isabella II pardoned most of the Americans soon after their arrival at Ceuta. This royal clemency was largely due to the efforts of President Millard Fillmore, who interceded in their behalf. A few others managed to escape from the penal colony at Ceuta, including a Hungarian, Louis Schlessinger, who always seemed to be on the losing side. He had fought with the patriot Kossuth in the unsuccessful insurrection of 1848 in Hungary and in 1856 he was destined to lose a battle in Costa Rica so quickly that William Walker would declare him a traitor. A major on the Bahia Honda invasion staff, Schlessinger later loyally denied the widely circulated report that Narciso López had carried a red rawhide whip in his hand during the battle of Las Pozas, which he vigorously applied to the shoulders of those filibuster soldiers who in his opinion were not firing their weapons fast enough.

Crittenden's last letter was printed in the *New Orleans Bee* on September 3, 1851, along with the tragic news of the execution of the fifty other filibusters. Outbursts of public indignation against Spain occurred throughout the United States, but mostly in the South. This nationwide rage was all the more intense because the Spanish commander of the steamer *Habanero* deliberately fired on the American ship *Falcon* at Bahia Honda at the very moment Crittenden was being executed.

Throughout New Orleans there resounded an overwhelming clamor for revenge against Spain. The *New Orleans Courier* even displayed the flag of the United States with the name CUBA emblazoned on it. A *Courier* editorial proclaimed: "American blood has been shed. It cries aloud for vengeance—vengeance on the tyrant . . . blood for blood! Our brethren must be avenged! Cuba must be seized!"

Serious riots broke out in New Orleans, and for several days there was talk of an armed expedition of revenge against Spanish Cuba. But after the news was received a few days later that López's forces had been completely routed and their leader executed, the press and the public in the South gradually calmed down.

The valiant Crittenden, however, was not soon forgotten. Several poems were composed and dedicated to the memory of this intrepid warrior from Kentucky. The following two stanzas are excerpted from "The Death of Crittenden," by Laura Lorimer; these verses were set to music and were very popular in the South during the 1850s:

THE DEATH OF CRITTENDEN

The flush of a tropical morn
   Still lingered on Cuba's fair sky,
When a band for chivalry born
   Were led forth like caitiffs to die.
No quiver on lips that had learned
   To press back each feeling that rose,
Told of thoughts in their bosoms inurned
   As their young lives drew near their sad close.

They bade the proud chief of that band
   Kneel low when the death volley came,
And, bowed on that sun-guarded strand,
   Pour forth his high spirit of flame;
Deep and haughty arose his firm tone,
   Unchecked by surroundings of woe,
"I kneel to high heaven alone,
   And ne'er turn my back on the foe!"

The Southern proslavery expansionists continued to attempt to obtain Cuba, but by diplomacy or purchase, rather than by filibustering. In 1854, during the administration of Franklin Pierce, the Ostend Manifesto was issued, proclaiming to the world that the United States was willing to purchase Cuba from Spain and hinting that if the island could not be bought there was a strong possibility of our using force to acquire it. But Spain would not part with the island, and after Narciso López no significant organized group from the United States invaded Cuba until the Spanish-American War of 1898.

4

The Misfortunes of Count Raousset-Boulbon and Henry A. Crabb in Sonora

FOLLOWING the disastrous failure of López in Cuba, one would think the ardor for filibustering for the national aggrandizement of the United States would have cooled. The virus, however, only spread westward.

When gold was discovered in California in 1848 an impetuous, reckless breed of men were attracted to the Golden State. Most had been lured by hopes of bonanza; others were trying to forget sorrow or failure elsewhere. After a while the constant pursuit of gambling, elusive wealth, prostitutes, brawling, and drink no longer satisfied many of these hardened adventurers. Filibusterism, looked on as a manly profession, had a definite appeal to tough "losers," despite (or perhaps because of) the risks involved. It was in keeping with the times: some dreamed of a successful private military undertaking in Latin America, which would lead to instant riches from an imaginary gold mine, or thought they might return as wealthy heroes—men of accomplishment to be admired by the general public. Little consideration was given to the more likely outcome of filibustering—that of becoming hated outlaws who would be hunted down, captured, and ruthlessly executed in a foreign land. Filibustering was a precarious and desperate gamble, not for the fainthearted.

The new boundary between Mexico and the United States, created by the Treaty of Guadalupe Hidalgo in 1848 at the conclusion of the Mexican War, had doubled the length of the border between the two countries. Formerly the Rio Grande

27

APACHE INDIANS ATTACKING SETTLERS IN SONORA

had been the main frontier; now the boundary extended along the Gila River all the way to the Pacific Ocean, traversing rough, half-desert terrain occupied by hostile Apache and Comanche Indian tribes who were unwilling to submit to either nation.

According to the treaty of 1848, the United States was supposed to police this lengthy frontier and keep the Indians in check. The border was much too long, however, for the American military authorities to maintain effective control.

The Apaches were especially troublesome in the northern part of the Mexican state of Sonora (part of which is now Arizona), where they brutally attacked ranches, mines, and haciendas, murdered innocent settlers, captured defenseless women and children, stole horses and cattle, disrupted the mining of gold and silver, and nearly wiped out the strictly rural population. Like the Americans, the Mexican military forces were unable to cope with the Apaches. The Mexican government therefore encouraged immigration from Europe—Anglo-Americans were excluded—in an effort to develop civilian frontier colonies.

Various Frenchmen attempted unsuccessfully to colonize northern Mexico. Hippolyte du Pasquier de Dommartin sought authorization from the Mexican government in 1851 to bring more than 100,000 immigrants from France to Chihuahua and Sonora; the idea was that large French colonies would assist Mexico in checking Yankee imperialism. Dommartin's efforts were in vain, and his grandiose colonization grants were never officially ratified by the central governmental authorities in Mexico. In the meantime, he spent so much money promoting his plans that he was ruined financially.

Even so, Dommartin may have been lucky: another intrepid French adventurer, Charles de Pindray, attracted by the lure of mineral wealth, attempted in 1852 to form a frontier French colony with 150 recruits in the valley of Cocóspera, in northern Sonora. The Apaches attacked the expedition and stole their horses. Supplies were cut off. De Pindray himself was mysteriously murdered—some suggested at the instigation of local Mexican authorities, who were suspicious of him.

Thousands of Frenchmen also came to San Francisco in the early 1850s in search of easy affluence. French wines and preserved fruits brought very high prices in the mining areas, while freight vessels from Europe provided reasonable transportation for fortune-seekers. Among this group was a ruined French nobleman, Count Gaston Raoul de Raousset-Boulbon.

Raousset-Boulbon was the eldest son of an ancient and venerated French family of Avignon. An unruly, uncontrollable youth, he was known at school as the "wolf cub." Restless and reckless, he squandered the fortune left him by his parents. Following unsuccessful business ventures in North Africa and England, he decided to try his luck in California.

The count was attracted by the lucre to be had from the goldfields but not by the arduous labor of a common miner. He wanted unlimited wealth and power but no rough work. For two years he lived by his wits in the neighborhood of San Francisco—hunting, fishing, trading cattle, and gambling. During this period he met Charles de Pindray and heard about the grandiose Gallic colonization schemes for Sonora, not to mention the remunerative possibilities of silver mining in Mexico.

Financed by the Franco-Mexican banking firm of Jecker-Torre, the count formed a mining corporation to be known as the Compañía Restauradora de la Mina de la Arizona. The company's prospects were indeed bright, for the silver deposits of the mountain range in northern Sonora to be exploited were legendary: the silver ore was said to be so pure that it could be readily scooped up in large *bolas* or nuggets.

This ambitious project was supposedly going to entail not only mining, but also trading, colonization, and, if necessary, pacification of the Apaches. Some two hundred recruits from San Francisco were enlisted in mid-1852. Almost all of them were French, and there were no Anglo-Americans because of the Mexican law forbidding them to colonize there.

In addition to the glittering metallic lure of Sonora, Count Raousset-Boulbon, as a loyal citizen of France, was interested in interrupting and blocking the progress of Manifest Destiny, which seemed to be pushing the United States ever southward toward Mexico. He asserted:

> Europeans are disturbed by the growth of the United States and rightly so. Unless she be dismembered, unless a powerful rival be built up beside her, America will become, through her commerce, her trade, her population, her geographical position upon two oceans, the inevitable mistress of the world. In ten years Europe dare not fire a shot without her permission. Voilà les États-Unis.

The French expedition landed at Guaymas on June 1, 1852, in an arrogant manner, with the full military pomp of a victorious army rather than as peaceful colonizers. The pretentious Raousset-Boulbon quickly made enemies in Mexico, since he liked to refer to himself as the "sultan of Sonora." After six weeks at the frontier the count tired of colonizing and, having found very little silver, decided to try his hand at political intrigue—pitting one local Mexican official against another. The net result was that the Sonoran Congress abrogated all mining claims of the Compañía Restauradora and appropriated funds for a military campaign, without further delay, against the so-called French colonizers. Raousset-Boulbon and his followers

COUNT GASTON RAOUSSET-BOULBON (1817–54)

An adventurer from France who attempted to organize a French filibustering expedition in Sonora, Mexico. The scheme failed and the count was executed by a Mexican firing squad at Guaymas in August 1854.

were informed they could stay in Sonora only if they renounced their French nationality and became citizens of Mexico; as a special concession, some fifty might remain in Sonora as French-men, but only as common laborers. These terms were immedi-ately rejected.

The French filibusters now put aside thoughts of colonization and started a military campaign with the objective of capturing Hermosillo, the largest town in the state of Sonora, with a popu-lation of about twelve thousand. The French met with initial success at Hermosillo: their charging cavalry caused the *nacio-nales* to flee in disorder. But General Miguel Blanco, who was in charge of the Mexican defenders, rounded up additional re-cruits and trained a Mexican cavalry unit that soon retaliated.

Time favored the Mexicans. Before long rampant diarrhea and amoebic dysentery took its toll of the Gallic invaders; many French soldiers became ill, and Raousset-Boulbon suffered such a serious attack that he had to be carried on a stretcher toward Guaymas. Surrounded by superior forces, the French soon lost their enthusiasm for battle. They surrendered to General Blanco on November 4, 1852, and were permitted to leave Sonora peacefully.

The count returned to San Francisco, claiming that he had failed because of poor health. He was pleased to note that he had become famous. Lionized as the "hero of Hermosillo," he proclaimed in the style of a full-fledged filibuster: "Sonora is condemned to sterility, to barbarism, and to be a desert unless a powerful interest will colonize it, and until the day when cannon-shots will open its ports to liberty. Sonora can become productive only through conquest." The count was still de-termined to establish a new Algeria in northern Mexico.

In 1853 Raousset-Boulbon went back to Mexico City, hoping to be rewarded with another mining and colonization concession in Sonora. The wily and suspicious Mexican president, Santa Anna, however, turned down the count's proposals, and the French leader, frustrated and resentful, was obliged to return to San Francisco.

In January 1854 President Santa Anna decided to allow

French, Belgian, Spanish, and other non-Anglo-Saxons in California to volunteer to come to northern Mexico as settlers. In this way he hoped to lure would-be French soldiers away from Raousset-Boulbon.

Some 480 of these volunteers, to be known as the French Battalion, went down to Guaymas in May 1854. Raousset-Boulbon himself arrived secretly in Guaymas in early July, taking with him a substantial amount of rifles and ammunition for the newly arrived "colonizers," who were biding their time and awaiting the count's instructions.

When General José María Yañez, the supreme commander of the Department of Sonora, learned of the hostile intentions of Raousset-Boulbon, he ordered all the French to leave Mexico immediately. The French Battalion rejected this unfriendly notification and proceeded to attack the Mexican army headquarters in Sonora on July 13, 1854.

The Mexican defenders had obtained a copy of the French battle plan, which had carelessly fallen into their possession, and were ready and waiting. Despite the valiant efforts of Raousset-Boulbon, the French invaders were decimated in a three-hour battle. Some forty-eight Frenchmen were killed, the rest wounded or captured. Most of the survivors were deported to Martinique.

The count himself was court-martialed, convicted of conspiracy to overthrow the Mexican government, and sentenced to death. He behaved with courage and serenity during his last days, writing farewell letters to his family and friends in France. He expressed his sincere appreciation to General Yañez for the privilege of being allowed to die with honor, without being humiliated—that is, standing, facing the firing squad, with his hands unbound, and with no blindfold. At sunrise on August 12, 1854, on the beach near Guaymas, a volley of Mexican musketry ended the stormy, romantic career of the daring French adventurer Count Gaston de Raousset-Boulbon, at the age of thirty-six. Following this debacle and his death, French filibustering and adventuring in inhospitable Sonora came to an end.

Although the French had learned their lesson, some intrepid American adventurers, including Henry Alexander Crabb, were still attracted to Sonora, apparently unconvinced that it was a death trap for filibusters of all nationalities.

Crabb, a contemporary of William Walker's, was also a native of Nashville, Tennessee. By profession a lawyer, he came to California in 1850 and was quite successful in local politics, being elected to the California state Senate. Fanatically pro-slavery in his views, he was defeated when he tried to become a United States senator from California. His ambitious dreams of political success in the Golden State having been shattered, his thoughts gravitated south of the border to the temptingly rich mineral treasures of Sonora. He had married into the commercially prominent Ainsa family of Sonora and California; through his Mexican in-laws, Crabb met and became involved in a political conspiracy with an intriguing revolutionary politico named Ignacio Pesqueira. The latter allegedly wanted to get rid of Governor Manuel M. Gándara of Sonora, so that he himself could take over this lucrative post. In return for Crabb's intervention with armed filibusters (posing as colonizers) against Gandara, Pesqueira promised the American some advantageous mining concessions in northern Sonora.

In late March 1857 Crabb crossed the border into Mexican territory at a point near Sonoyta with some ninety footloose adventurers. The group, known as the Arizona Colonization Company, headed southeast along the arid, treacherous Camino del Diablo toward the village of Caborca. Dry arroyos, sparse mesquite, sharp cacti, and the threat of hostile Apaches and Mexican outlaws offered little hospitality to the visitors. Crabb was confident, however, since he counted on the support of his friend Pesqueira.

Meanwhile, Pesqueira had other ideas. Unbeknownst to Crabb, Pesqueira had overthrown Gándara, gained political control of Sonora, and no longer needed Crabb's help. On the contrary, Crabb had now become an embarrassing liability that might cause trouble with the federal Mexican government. Pesqueira, instead of welcoming the Americans as fellow con-

HENRY A. CRABB (1823–57)
Another gringo filibuster who led an ill-fated "colonization" expedition
into Sonora, Mexico. He was captured by the Mexicans in April 1857,
in the village of Caborca, and brutally executed. His severed head
was preserved in an earthenware jar filled with vinegar as a warning
to North Americans to stay out of Mexico.

spirators, turned against them. He issued a proclamation to all patriotic Sonorans to arm themselves in preparation for a bloody battle to free Mexico from the invading gringos. He declared: "Viva Mexico! Death to the Filibusters. Show no mercy to this horde of pirates. Kill them."

In early April the Mexicans attacked Crabb and his followers in a wheat field near Caborca. After suffering severe casualties, some forty-four Americans took refuge in a large straw-thatched adobe building on the main plaza (square) of the town. During a six-day siege about fifteen hundred Mexicans converged on Caborca and surrounded it. A flame-tipped arrow set fire to the thatched roof of Crabb's stronghold.

Their position hopeless, the embattled Americans asked the Mexicans for terms of surrender. The Mexican commander promised medical care for the wounded and fair treatment for the survivors. The gringos accepted these terms and came out unarmed to give themselves up. Thereupon they were all bound, marched into a nearby barracks, sentenced to death, and shot at sunrise on April 7, 1857. Only one, a sixteen-year-old boy named Charles Evans, was spared and lived to tell the tale of woe.

The American corpses were left unburied to putrefy in the sun and were fed to the local hogs.

Following the ruthless mass execution, Crabb's head was cut off and preserved for many months in a large earthenware jar filled with vinegar. From time to time this grim trophy would be displayed in the main plaza of Caborca to celebrate a courageous victory and serve as a sinister warning to other North American filibusters to stay away.

The ill-fated temptation of filibustering in Latin America that attracted López, Crittenden, Raousset-Boulbon, and Crabb to calamitous doom was about to entice William Walker.

5

Walker's Fiasco in
Lower California and Sonora

THE New Orleans *Daily Crescent* changed ownership in February 1850. William Walker decided to join a host of other restless spirits and move to California. He arrived in San Francisco on July 21, 1850, on the steamship *Oregon*, having made the trip from New Orleans via Panama. Walker soon found employment as an editor of the *San Francisco Daily Herald*.

Before long his newly acquired aggressive tactics got him into trouble with two San Francisco judges in separate incidents. In an editorial in January 1851 Walker implied in no uncertain terms that a certain probate judge named Morrison had illegally misappropriated funds from the estate of a deceased foreigner that had been entrusted to him—suggesting indeed that the judge, instead of "preserving" the deceased's estate, had "pickled" it. This offensive innuendo so infuriated the judge that he arranged to have a sharpshooting employee of his named Will Hicks Graham challenge William Walker to a duel with revolvers at eight paces. During the ensuing affair of honor, Walker was shot twice: first in the trousers and then superficially in the fleshy part of his thigh. Graham got through it all unscathed and unscratched, and there the matter ended.

Undaunted by this close call, Walker soon became involved in a feud with the public administrator of San Francisco, Judge Levi Parsons. The San Francisco underworld had started many fires in that city, destroying some twenty blocks of wooden buildings—including the printing establishment of the *Herald*.

EMIGRATION TO
CALIFORNIA !

Do you want to go to California? If so, go and join the Company who intend going out the middle of March, or 1st of April next, under the charge of the California Emigration Society, in a first-rate Clipper Ship. The Society agreeing to find places for all those who wish it upon their arrival in San Francisco. The voyage will probably be made in a few months.— Price of passage will be in the vicinity of

ONE HUNDRED DOLLARS !
CHILDREN IN PROPORTION.

A number of families have already engaged passage. A suitable Female Nurse has been provided, who will take charge of Young Ladies and Children. Good Physicians, both male and female go in the Ship. It is hoped a large number of females will go, as Females are getting almost as good wages as males.

FEMALE NURSES get 25 dollars per week and board. SCHOOL TEACHERS 100 dollars per month. GARDNERS 60 dollars per month and board. LABORERS 4 to 5 dollars per day. BRICKLAYERS 6 dollars per day. HOUSEKEEPERS 40 dollars per month. FARMERS 5 dollars per day. SHOEMAKERS 4 dollars per day. Men and Women COOKS 40 to 60 dollars per month and board. MINERS are making from 3 to 12 dollars per day. FEMALE SERVANTS 30 to 50 dollars per month and board. Washing 3 dollars per dozen. MASONS 6 dollars per day. CARPENTERS 5 dollars per day. ENGINEERS 100 dollars per month, and as the quartz Crushing Mills are getting into operation all through the country, Engineers are very scarce. BLACKSMITHS 90 and 100 dollars per month and board.

IN 1850 WILLIAM WALKER, ALONG WITH MANY OTHER ADVENTUROUS SPIRITS, EMIGRATED TO CALIFORNIA

THE PORT OF GUAYMAS—SONORA, MEXICO

According to William Walker, the territory of Sonora, including this port, should have been acquired by the United States to provide an outlet for the American southwest on the Gulf of California.

Walker wrote a derisive, vitriolic editorial entitled "The Press Is a Nuisance," in which he accused Judge Parsons of being too lenient with criminals. Parsons was so outraged by this uncalled-for insinuation that he cited William Walker for contempt of court, sentenced him to jail, and fined him five hundred dollars. This episode made Walker quite a local hero in San Francisco. Some four thousand irate citizens gathered in March 1851 in a public square near the prison and called for three cheers for Walker and three groans for Judge Parsons. After six days the Superior Court judges released Walker from jail, although he eventually had to pay the fine.

Soon after this incident Walker abandoned San Francisco for the town of Marysville, California, where he returned to the legal profession as a partner of Henry P. Watkins. The law was too quiet and boring, however, for his impatient and turbulent nature. After Ellen Martin's death he had gradually come to feel that he had a mission in life, as if he had had a revelation from God that he was destined to accomplish some important task—perhaps as a crusader against evil and ignorance. While still working for the *Daily Crescent* in New Orleans in 1849, Walker had written an editorial praising the Polish general Józef Bem, who had joined the Hungarian army as a revolutionary and with a small force had waged a brilliant campaign in that year to defeat a numerically superior Austrian army. Perhaps now Walker's thoughts turned once again to Bem; possibly for the first time he visualized himself as an American military leader who might win great and just battles south of the border.

The newspapers in San Francisco began to commiserate with the unfortunate citizens of Sonora and suggested that United States troops, for humanitarian reasons, occupy the area and protect the settlers from the terrorizing raids of the Apache Indians. In September 1853 the San Francisco newspaper *Alta California* published a sensational account of the frightful Apache outrages: the Indians had murdered eighty citizens of Sonora in a single week.

At the same time, the press pointed out that things in Sonora weren't all bad: there was, for example, fabulous mineral wealth —silver deposits that could be exploited most economically.

William Walker became interested in a scheme to colonize Sonora and Lower California. Impatient for action, he first attempted to cooperate with Count Raousset-Boulbon, but the latter pointed out that North American gringos were so detested in Mexico that Walker's offered assistance was impractical and unwanted.

Walker then decided to strike out on his own, as a rival of the French. In July 1853, having been duly provided with the necessary passport visa, granted by the Mexican vice-consul in San Francisco, he visited the small, hot, dusty seaport of Guay-

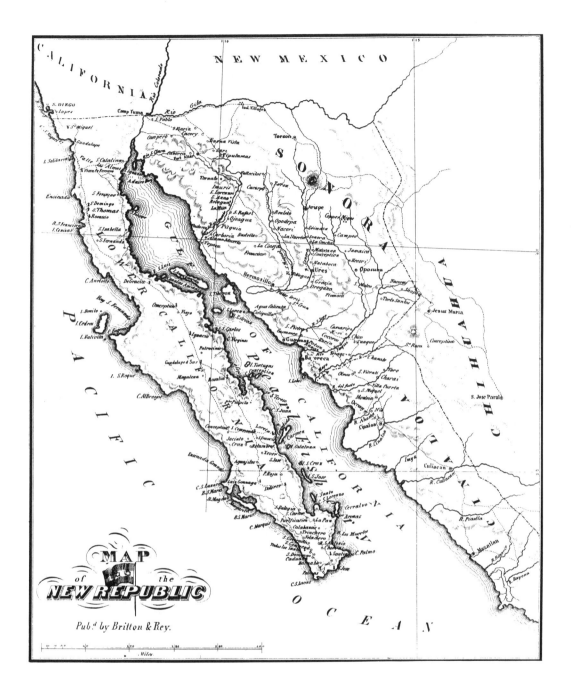

SONORA AND LOWER CALIFORNIA

Mexican territory invaded in vain by William Walker in his first filibustering expedition in 1853–54. The two stars on the small flag (lower left) represent the two Mexican states, Sonora and Lower California, that Walker intended to govern in his abortive new republic.

mas in Sonora, accompanied by his law partner, Henry P. Watkins. The port authorities in Guaymas had been warned about
Walker's visit by the Mexican consulate in San Francisco and
would not grant him permission to leave Guaymas to visit the
interior of Sonora, even though he claimed he merely wished to
inspect a tract of land with the idea of forming a proposed
Anglo-American mining colony. For almost a month Walker,
assisted by the American consul in Guaymas, Juan A. Robinson,
tried in vain to obtain this travel permit, but the Mexican officials
would not yield. After much fruitless bickering, Walker and
Watkins finally returned to San Francisco somewhat disgruntled.
During this period of enforced idleness, a world traveler and
author named T. Robinson Warren, who also happened to be in
Guaymas, got to know William Walker quite well and later
vividly described the incipient filibuster:

> To have looked at William Walker, one could scarcely have credited
> him to be the originator and prime mover of so desperate an enterprise
> as the invasion of the state of Sonora.
> His appearance was that of anything else than a military chieftain.
> Below the medium height, and very slim, I should hardly imagine
> him to weigh over a hundred pounds. His hair light and towy, while
> his almost white eyebrows and lashes concealed a seemingly pupilless,
> grey, cold eye, and his face was a mass of yellow freckles, the whole
> expression very heavy. His dress was scarcely less remarkable than
> his person. His head was surmounted by a huge white fur hat, whose
> long nap waved with the breeze, which, together with a very ill-made
> short-waisted blue coat, with gilt buttons, and a pair of grey, strapless
> pantaloons, made up the ensemble of as unprepossessing-looking a
> person as one would meet in a day's walk. I will leave you to imagine
> the figure he cut in Guaymas with the thermometer at 100°, when
> every one else was arrayed in white. Indeed, half the dread which the
> Mexicans had of filibusters vanished when they saw this their Grand
> Sachem,—such an insignificant-looking specimen. But any one who
> estimated Mr. Walker by his personal appearance, made a great mis-
> take. Extremely taciturn, he would sit for an hour in company without
> opening his lips; but once interested, he arrested your attention with
> the first word he uttered, and as he proceeded, you felt convinced that
> he was no ordinary person.

Back in California, Walker was more convinced than ever that
if the Sonorans would not listen to reason it would be necessary
to form a filibustering expedition and apply force. Sonora would

CAPE SAN LUCAS WAS THE FIRST
BRIEF STOP IN WILLIAM WALKER'S
UNSUCCESSFUL INVASION OF LOWER
CALIFORNIA IN OCTOBER 1853

"THE USED-UP MAN"
Caricature of a disappointed, impoverished gold-seeker. Many vagrants of this
type became filibusters in the army of
William Walker.

PRESIDENT WALKER'S ARMY IN SONORA—WRITING DISPATCHES HOME.

WILLIAM WALKER'S FIRST FILIBUSTERING
EFFORT IN SONORA, MEXICO, IN 1853, RESULTED
IN FAILURE; FOR A FEW MONTHS WALKER
DECLARED HIMSELF PRESIDENT OF SONORA
BEFORE BEING DRIVEN OUT BY THE MEXICAN
CAVALRY

be invaded by American soldiers of fortune disguised as colonists, in an attempt to gain control of this Mexican state—either with or without the approbation of the Mexican government.

To raise money to recruit troops, purchase guns, ammunition, supplies, and charter a ship, bonds were sold in California, to be secured by the land that Walker's expedition was to acquire in Sonora. That Mexican state was to be conquered and declared an independent republic, preferably under the protection of the United States. A military colony would then be established on the frontier of Sonora to protect the citizens against Apache raids. The French contracts and mining concessions in Sonora were to be canceled and done away with, once and for all. The 1848 Treaty of Guadalupe Hidalgo ending the Mexican War had been disappointing to many American expansionists, who wanted the United States to annex even more of Mexico. So both Manifest Destiny and the Monroe Doctrine seemed to be on the side of Walker's filibusters.

In October 1853 Walker sailed from San Francisco on the brig *Caroline* with a ragtag army of forty-five recruits—actually reckless saloon loafers and the dregs of the California docks. A city-bred lawyer and physician, Walker, a self-appointed colonel, had never undergone any soldierly training and was totally unfamiliar with the military world of snarl and snap. From the very beginning his virgin martial effort was amateurish and destined to fail—a foolhardy piece of business. To get around United States neutrality laws and avoid possible seizure by the U. S. Army, the *Caroline* had to depart from San Francisco in such a hurry that most of the expedition's food and ammunition were left behind, to be seized by federal officers on the wharf.

The hasty departure of the *Caroline* also meant that Walker had not been able to gather as many men as he planned. Once he was at sea Walker realized that his force was too small to attack the strong Mexican garrison at Guaymas: what chance would he have with forty-five demoralized recruits to conquer a Mexican state which the year before had defeated Count de Raousset-Boulbon with several times that number of well-trained French filibusters? So he abruptly changed his plans: first the small expeditionary force would conquer the sparsely populated region of Lower California—the long, narrow, arid, remote peninsula across the Gulf of California from Sonora. Walker, after touching briefly at Cape San Lucas, landed at La Paz, made a prisoner of the astounded governor, hauled down the Mexican flag, and as the filibusters cheered replaced it with his own new red and white barred flag with two stars— emblematic of the states of Lower California and Sonora.

On November 3, 1853, William Walker proclaimed that Lower California was free, sovereign, and independent—and no longer owed any allegiance to Mexico. The lethargic inhabitants of La Paz were quite confused: they didn't know who the filibusters were or what they wanted. A new territorial governor arrived unexpectedly at La Paz, and he also was captured by the gringos.

A few days later Walker, who has been expecting reinforcements, decided not to wait any longer for them to arrive. He withdrew from La Paz and moved his headquarters up the coast to the more thickly populated northwestern region of Lower California, from which Sonora could be reached overland. The port of Ensenada, about eighty miles south of the United States border and conveniently situated for receiving fresh recruits, was selected as the new center of operations.

FORT McKIBBIN, NEAR ENSENADA, MEXICO

In December 1853 a young lieutenant in Walker's army named McKibbin was killed in action by the Mexicans. This fort was named in his honor.

At La Paz a brief skirmish had taken place between half a dozen of Walker's soldiers, who had gone ashore to gather wood, and some native inhabitants. Walker himself landed with some thirty additional filibusters to support his wood-gatherers and drove back a small Mexican force. A month later the *Alta California* blew up this incident into a glorious military victory, eulogizing the freeing of Lower California from the tyrannous yoke of decadent Mexico and endorsing the establishment of a new republic. Public sentiment in the United States seemed to be overwhelmingly in favor of Walker's filibusters.

On November 30, 1853, Colonel William Walker wrote from Ensenada a rhetorical proclamation directed to the people of the United States, clarifying his position in Lower California:

> In declaring the Republic of Lower California Free, Sovereign and Independent, I deem it proper to give the People of the United States the reasons for the course I have taken. It is due to the nationality which has most jealously guarded the Independence of American States, to declare why another Republic is created on the immediate confines of the Great Union.
>
> The Mexican Government has for a long time failed to perform its duties to the Province of Lower California. Cut off as the Territory was, by the treaty of Guadalupe Hidalgo from all direct communication with the rest of Mexico, the central authorities have manifested little or no interest in the affairs of the California Peninsula. The geographical position of the Province is such as to make it entirely separate and distinct in its interests from the other portions of the Mexican Republic. But the moral and social ties which bound it to Mexico, have been even weaker and more dissoluble than the physical. Hence, to develop the resources of Lower California, and to effect a proper social organization therein, it was necessary to make it Independent.
>
> On such considerations have I and my companions in arms acted in the course we have pursued. And for the success of our enterprise, we put our trust in Him who controls the destiny of nations, and guides them in the ways of progress and improvement.
>
> Wm. Walker, Col.,
President of Lower California

Eager volunteers flocked to the recruiting office at Kearney and Sacramento streets in San Francisco to enlist in Walker's army. A nation that had successfully pressed westward for three thousand miles should be strong enough to move south-ward. Perhaps world history was in the making. The spirit of war was in the air: first conquer Lower California, then on to Sonora! Hooray for Walker! Henry P. Watkins, the recruiting officer, soon had 230 spirited soldiers of fortune. They set out for Ensenada on the brig *Anita* with guns and ammunition but very little food.

In the meantime, Walker was running into a lot of trouble at Ensenada. The *Caroline* had been taken over by some Mexicans and had escaped, carrying the two Mexican governors and considerable supplies (apparently the ship's mate had been bribed by the Mexicans). To make matters worse, Walker's force was suddenly attacked by a horde of Mexican volunteers under the command of a notorious guerrilla fighter named Guadalupe Melendres. These Mexicans did not want to be "liberated," and killed several of the filibusters at the town of Santo Tomás, near Ensenada.

Faced with an acute shortage of rations, Walker sent Watkins back to California for a cargo of provisions. The troops at Ensenada soon tired of their meager diet of nothing but high-sounding pronouncements plus a little beef and corn that had been forcibly collected from nearby Mexican villages. The morale of the recruits, already weakened by idleness and dysentery, started to crack badly. Fifty mutinous soldiers revolted against Walker's authority, quit, and marched off in the general direction of San Diego.

Despite these harassing reversals, William Walker proclaimed himself president of Sonora on January 18, 1854, simultaneously declaring the newly founded republic of Sonora to be independent of Mexico. Furthermore, the republic was henceforth to be divided into two states: the state of Sonora and the state of Lower California. The Civil Code and the Code of Legal Practice of the state of Louisiana were to apply in the republic of Sonora. This was a bold stroke of the diminutive leader's most adept weapon, the pen, for his troops were still a long way from Sonora. Supported by a handful of men, he had arrogantly "taken possession" of two Mexican states without the knowledge or consent of the inhabitants he had "liberated."

The following eyewitness account from *Annals of San Francisco,* December 13, 1853, gives an insight into the attitude of Californians toward Walker's filibustering campaign in Lower California:

> When news of this short campaign reached San Francisco, there was a mighty ado with the friends and sympathizers of the expedition. Among the few initiated in the supposed secret causes of the adventure, there were brilliant hopes of the indefinite extension of one of the peculiar "domestic institutions" [slavery] of the South, and among all were glorious dreams of conquest and plunder. The national flag of the new Republic was run up at the corner of Kearny and Sacramento streets, and an office was opened for the purpose of enlisting recruits. The excitement was great in the city. At the corners of the streets and in barrooms, groups of intending buccaneers and their friends collected, and discussed the position of affairs. More volunteers appeared than there were means of conveying to the scene of action.
>
> News next reached the city of the *battle* near Santo Tomás, where the filibusters, when said to be in the act of helping themselves to the cattle and provisions of the natives were severely handled, and a few of them slain. This, however, only fired the recruits the more to help their oppressed brethren. Why could not the Lower Californians, poor, ignorant brutes have been contented with the beautiful scrip of the new Republic for their paltry provisions? The rage for war—freedom to the Mexicans, death to the Apaches, and plunder to the Americans—spread over all California, and numbers hastened from the mining regions to San Francisco, to depart southward in time and share in the spoil of the conquered land. . . . The newspapers recorded their various movements at length, and in general either indirectly praised, or did not strongly condemn them.
>
> People in private circles laughed, and talked over the business coolly. They generally thought, and said, it was all right—at all events, it was a fine specimen of the go-aheadism of Young America. Moneyed men even advanced considerable sums for the use of the expeditionists, and the scrip of the new Republic was almost saleable on 'Change, at a dime for a dollar.
>
> We have mentioned this affair at some length, more to show the general wild and reckless character of the people, and the state of public opinion upon filibustering, in San Francisco, and in California at large, than to chronicle the particular doings of the adventurers. Our people are mostly in the prime of life, their passions are of the strongest, they have an acute intellect, absolute will and physical strength, but they are not distinguished by high moral and political principle. They are sanguine in whatever things they undertake, and are more inclined to desperate deeds, than to the peaceful business of ordinary life.

Had Walker's party succeeded in reaching Sonora and been able to stand their own [ground] for a time or perhaps signally to defeat the Mexicans in a pitched battle, ten thousand of our mixed Californians would have hastened to their triple-striped two-star standard. Against such a force not all the power of Mexico would have been sufficient to dislodge the invaders from Sonora. Other tens of thousands would have flocked into the country, and perforce it would have been thoroughly Americanized. Undoubtedly this will happen some day. Is it not "manifest destiny"? People here certainly look upon it as such, and hence very little fault has been found, in general, with the proceedings of the filibusters. The principles of action now existing in California, in so far at least as regards neighboring countries, are something like those of Wordsworth's hero, who acted upon

"The good old rule, the simple plan—
That they should take who have the power,
And they should keep who can."

Walker's expedition to Lower California, sometimes described as an opéra bouffe, was destined to end in forlorn disaster. Politically it may have been of some importance, however, since the Mexican government may have believed that the United States government was supporting Walker (although the opposite was, in fact, the case). If so, this misunderstanding had significant consequences.

In December 1853 James Gadsden, the American minister to Mexico, was attempting to convince that country to sell a strip of land in northern Sonora to the United States to be the site of a transcontinental railroad. Mexican officials thought the price offered was too low. William Walker's activities in Lower California, however, may possibly have convinced them that the United States would attempt to take Sonora by force, without any compensation, if other negotiations failed. In any event, a treaty was hastily drawn up and signed on December 31, 1853. Known as the Gadsden Purchase, it enabled the United States to acquire the northern part of Sonora (approximately thirty thousand square miles), including portions of the mineral-rich territories of Arizona and New Mexico, for the modest price of $10 million. The United States government also committed itself to preventing Apache raids into Mexican territory. Gadsden wrote a letter to the Mexican government to the effect that the United States regarded William Walker as a violator of

BONDS WERE SOLD IN CALIFORNIA IN 1853 TO RAISE MONEY FOR
WALKER'S FILIBUSTERING EXPEDITION IN SONORA

federal law, to be dealt with accordingly. Thus Walker lost all
hope of active support from the United States government.

To this day it is not clear whether Walker's activities in
Sonora in 1853 helped Gadsden in his negotiations with the
Mexican government or merely embarrassed and hindered the
American minister.

In early February 1854 a Mexican war vessel standing by in
the port of Ensenada was soon joined by the U.S.S. *Portsmouth*
—both ships intent on observing the activities of the filibuster
army. Walker now decided to move out: he ordered his small
battery of fieldpieces to be spiked and with about 135 men
marched away from Ensenada across the narrow peninsula in
the general direction of Sonora. He hoped to stir up an insurrection against the Mexican government so that the Gulf of

GUADALUPE PASS, SONORA
William Walker's disastrous filibustering invasion of Sonora, Mexico
in 1853–54 came to grief on rugged trails such as these.

California could be added to the disappointing Gadsden Purchase and thus provide the United States with a much-needed (in Walker's opinion) coastal outlet for the American southwest.

In the nearby village of San Vicente, once prosperous but now abandoned because of Apache raids, Walker made a final effort to rally some Mexicans to his cause. He summoned a forced convention of sixty-two bewildered *rancheros* on February 28, 1854, and persuaded them, against a background of martial music, to take an oath of allegiance to the new republic of Sonora.

The courtyard of the crumbling old mission was selected as the site for the ceremonial convention. A table was placed in the center of the weather-beaten patio, with two of Walker's new red-starred flags in front of it forming an arch. The Mexicans filed up to give their names, take the oath of allegiance, and pass under the bizarre flags. Many perplexed natives were not sure why they were there or what they were doing. Those who hesitated were gently prodded in the rear by a double line of armed gringos. After the whole local crowd had been "naturalized" many compliments and congratulations were exchanged, the troops gave three cheers, and weapons were fired in the air as a formal salute. A few brass horns accompanied the fusillade with appropriate blaring honks (some German filibusters had brought their trumpets along with them from California).

The next day Walker delivered the following impassioned address to this filibuster army, outlining the alleged motives of the Sonora military campaign:

SOLDIERS OF SONORA!

You are about to undertake a most glorious enterprise.—You start to cross the Colorado in order to defend a helpless people, from the attacks of merciless savages. For years the population of Sonora has been the prey of the Apache Indians. Their property has been taken from them—their wives and children have been massacred, or consigned to a captivity worse than death, by the torturing fire of a worthless foe. The men of Sonora have been forced to see their wives and daughters ravished—and babies at the breast have been torn from their mothers, and murdered before the eyes of captive parents. All these outrages, at which the civilization of the whole continent blushes, have been permitted by the Government which pretends to control the people of Sonora. Mexico has stood by, and her silence and inactivity, have so encouraged the Apache, that he now threatens to ride into Guaymas, and render the whole country from the mountains to the sea, subject to his savage will, and tributary to his bestial desires.

You, Soldiers! are now called upon to wrest the country from the rule of the Apache, and make it the abode of order and civilization. It is possible that in your chivalrous efforts you may be opposed by the Mexican government. If you are, when you meet the enemy, let the holiness of your cause, move your arms and strengthen your souls. When you strike at a Mexican foe, remember that you strike at an auxiliary of the Apache,—at an accessory to the murder of innocent children, and the rape of helpless women. Fill your minds with these ideas, and victory will follow you in the plains of Sonora. In such a cause, failure is impossible, and triumph certain. The God of battles is with you, and you will be strong, and prevail against a host of enemies.

(Signed) Wm. Walker,
Commander-in-chief of the Army of Sonora

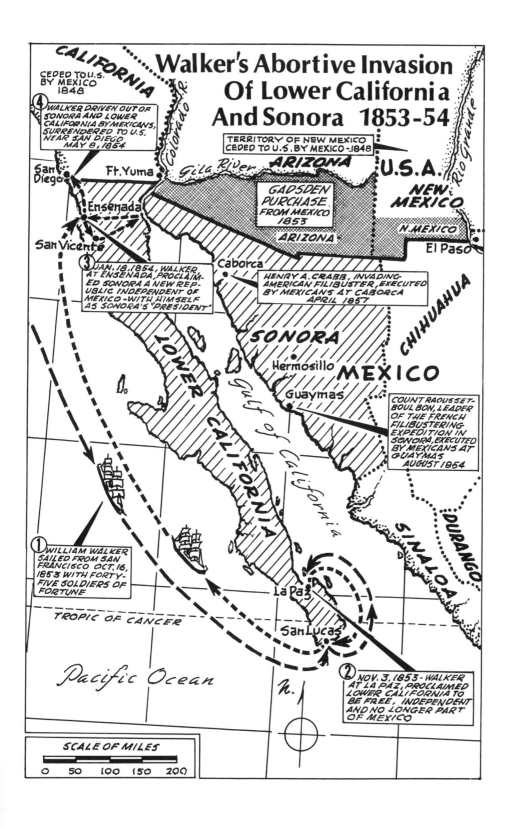

Walker's Abortive Invasion Of Lower California And Sonora 1853-54

CALIFORNIA

CEDED TO U.S. BY MEXICO 1848

④ WALKER DRIVEN OUT OF SONORA AND LOWER CALIFORNIA BY MEXICANS, SURRENDERED TO U.S. NEAR SAN DIEGO MAY 8, 1854

TERRITORY OF NEW MEXICO CEDED TO U.S. BY MEXICO - 1848

ARIZONA

U.S.A.

NEW MEXICO

GADSDEN PURCHASE FROM MEXICO 1853

ARIZONA

N. MEXICO

San Diego

Ft. Yuma

Gila River

Colorado R.

Rio Grande

Ensenada

El Paso

San Vicente

③ JAN. 18, 1854, WALKER AT ENSENADA, PROCLAIMED SONORA A NEW REPUBLIC INDEPENDENT OF MEXICO - WITH HIMSELF AS SONORA'S "PRESIDENT"

Caborca

HENRY A. CRABB, INVADING AMERICAN FILIBUSTER, EXECUTED BY MEXICANS AT CABORCA APRIL 1857

CHIHUAHUA

SONORA

Hermosillo

MEXICO

Guaymas

LOWER CALIFORNIA

Gulf of California

COUNT RAOUSSET-BOUL BON, LEADER OF THE FRENCH FILIBUSTERING EXPEDITION IN SONORA, EXECUTED BY MEXICANS AT GUAYMAS AUGUST 1854

SINALOA

DURANGO

① WILLIAM WALKER SAILED FROM SAN FRANCISCO OCT. 16, 1853 WITH FORTY-FIVE SOLDIERS OF FORTUNE

La Paz

TROPIC OF CANCER

San Lucas

Pacific Ocean

N.

② NOV. 3, 1853 - WALKER AT LA PAZ, PROCLAIMED LOWER CALIFORNIA TO BE FREE, INDEPENDENT AND NO LONGER PART OF MEXICO

SCALE OF MILES

0   50   100   150   200

In spite of this fervent pep talk, lack of food, discontent, sickness, and open mutiny weakened the filibuster army. Further desertions took place. Walker learned of a plot by ten of his soldiers to blow up the ammunition and seize all available food and supplies during the confusion. He immediately arrested two of the ringleaders and had them summarily shot by a firing squad; other troublemakers were whipped and drummed out of camp. Even though the number of Americans was small and diminishing day by day, Walker did not hesitate: he looked upon a military execution as a good test of the soldierly discipline of his troops. For the first time Walker showed the fanatical insistence on harsh punishment that was later to make his name a symbol of terror in Central America.

Leaving a garrison of twenty men to guard his headquarters at San Vicente, he set out with about a hundred recruits to drive a herd of cattle over the rugged, stony unknown trails of the sierras to the mouth of the Colorado River—a wearisome march of some two hundred miles through desolate country. By the time they arrived at the river most of the men were in rags, their boots worn through. To reach Sonora, they were now faced with the grim prospect of crossing the deep, swirling current. The men managed to pass across safely on makeshift wooden rafts, but the frightened cattle, driven into the river, were all swept away and drowned.

The filibusters had finally reached the promised land of Sonora, but their situation was utterly hopeless: they were starving and half naked, in a barren wasteland of sagebrush, sand, and rocks. About fifty men deserted on the spot and started the northward trek upstream to Fort Yuma, some seventy miles away, just over the United States boundary. Walker decided to lead the rest of his bedraggled troops back to San Vicente to rescue the comrades who had been left at the post. In the middle of April their reluctant retreat brought the filibusters back into San Vicente—only to find to their horror that Melendres and his hostile followers had massacred the small garrison.

Melendres and the Mexicans now closed in on Walker's forlorn band and harassed them relentlessly by sniping, day and night. Walker proudly (and probably wisely) rejected a Mexican offer to allow the filibusters to retreat peacefully, provided they would lay down their arms.

May 8, 1854, was William Walker's thirtieth birthday. By this time his personal hiking equipment had been reduced to one dilapidated boot. Under a hot desert sun Walker and thirty-three parched, dejected, and limping soldiers of fortune staggered toward the California town of Tía Juana. But Melendres and his jeering, mounted Mexicans had placed themselves between the oncoming filibusters and the boundary separating Mexico and the United States. The filibuster leader ordered his men to charge, and with ferocious yells they plunged forward at the tormenting Mexicans, who wavered, then broke ranks and galloped off southward.

Once across the border, the erstwhile president of the republic of Sonora approached two U. S. Army officers who had been waiting near San Diego, saluted, and announced with military dignity: "I am Colonel William Walker. I wish to surrender my force to the United States." The thirty-four filibusters pledged their word of honor to report in San Francisco to undergo trial for their violation of the federal neutrality laws. Five months later, in October 1854, Walker's trial took place.

Edmund Randolph served as Walker's attorney, although Walker, being a lawyer, defended himself quite effectively. He pointed out that owing to interference by the United States government he had been forced to put to sea on the *Caroline* with only forty-five men (instead of a much larger number of recruits) and had been deprived of needed supplies and ammunition. He and his followers had been obliged to change their plans while at sea, and land in a sparsely settled region where they had to raise some kind of a flag. They were able to survive many hardships, knowing right and humanity were on their side—for after all they had wanted to rescue the people of Sonora from a corrupt government and protect them against the raids of the ferocious Apaches. Like the Pilgrim fathers, he had come to a savage land to rescue it from savages and make it a safe abode for civilization.

The federal prosecutor scoffed at Walker's so-called humane views and made it quite clear that Walker was guilty of violating the neutrality laws. The judge, in his summation to the jury, also took a stand highly unfavorable to Walker.

But the jury had a different point of view. After only eight minutes of deliberation they returned a verdict of not guilty. When Walker was acquitted the United States government dropped the cases against the other minor soldiers of fortune who had been with him in Sonora. It was quite apparent that "the Filibuster"—an epithet often applied to William Walker—and the concept of Manifest Destiny enjoyed tremendous popular support.

THE HEIGHT OF ARROGANCE In this document of surrender to U.S. authorities signed near the Mexican border in California on May 8, 1854, Walker was presumptuous enough to designate himself "President of the Republic of Sonora," whereas in reality he was a frustrated, defeated soldier of fortune.

6

Cornelius Vanderbilt and the Transit Route

DURING the sixteenth century Spanish engineers in the New World informed their sovereigns that three main routes across Middle America were feasible: through Panama, through Nicaragua, and across the Isthmus of Tehuantepec in Mexico. They suggested that a waterway be cut through the Isthmus of Panama for the future glory of Spain. The Spanish never got beyond the preliminary surveys for a canal, however, and for three hundred years the project lay dormant. Then on January 24, 1848, gold was discovered at Sutter's Mill in California. The neglected, half-forgotten western coast of America suddenly became the promised land.

Central America immediately became important to world commerce as the logical site for a canal that would unite the Atlantic and Pacific oceans and cut short the distance to the goldfields. Before the opening of a transcontinental railroad across the United States in 1869, the overland trip to California from the eastern seaboard was prolonged, arduous, and often dangerous, owing to attacks by hostile Indians and bandits. For people living near the Gulf of Mexico or the Atlantic Ocean, passage to California by ship seemed to be the most desirable choice. One could, of course, make the all-water voyage around Cape Horn, but it was a stormy, seemingly interminable route. The crossing at Tehuantepec was quite popular about 1850, but it entailed a land passage of at least 130 miles. This Mexican route gradually declined in importance, for the routes through

IN 1850 MANY TRAVELERS PREFERRED THE VOYAGE FROM NEW YORK TO THE WEST VIA THE NICARAGUA TRANSIT LINE RATHER THAN THE FORMIDABLE OVERLAND ROUTE TO CALIFORNIA

Panama and Nicaragua, utilizing lakes and rivers, necessitated traversing much shorter strips of land: in Panama about twenty-eight miles and in Nicaragua only some twelve miles.

After a railroad was completed through the jungles of Panama in 1855, passengers could cross the isthmus from ocean to ocean in half a day. During the 1850s the Panama route was the most popular way for passengers to travel between the Atlantic and Pacific coasts of the United States, although it was challenged for a few years by the shorter, cheaper, and healthier Nicaragua route. Since Nicaragua's latitude was higher, the climate was said to be cooler, and passengers were less exposed to the risk of tropical fevers.

Nicaragua was one of the five Central American republics (the others were Guatemala, El Salvador, Honduras, and Costa Rica) that had achieved independence from Spain in 1821.

These five countries were loosely joined together in the Federation of Central America from 1823 to 1839, when they separated into independent republics. Sectional political feuds, lack of communication, and the conflict between church and state contributed to the dissolution of the federation.

More attention had been given to Nicaragua than to Panama as the prospective site for a canal. The route by way of Nicaragua was shorter: through Panama it was 5,245 miles from New York to San Francisco, while it was only 4,871 miles via Nicaragua. An engineering system for lifting vessels had not yet been perfected in the middle of the nineteenth century, so the fact that a canal across Panama would necessitate an elevation far above sea level was another point in Nicaragua's favor. It was more feasible and would require fewer locks to dig a canal that would connect the Pacific Ocean and Lake Nicaragua, where it would join the San Juan River and go on to the Caribbean. A lock canal constructed between the Pacific port of San Juan del Sur and Lake Nicaragua would not only have the advantage of traversing a very narrow strip of land but also would cross at the lowest point in the whole continental divide between the Arctic and Cape Horn—an elevation of only about 150 feet above sea level.

By 1849 various studies had been made of the practicability of such a Nicaraguan canal. This giant undertaking attracted the attention of an astute and resourceful financier, Cornelius Vanderbilt of New York. Vanderbilt was fifty-five years of age. As a poor boy of sixteen he had started as a humble ferryman, but through ability, energy, luck, and ruthless persistence he had built up a huge operation of ferries, river steamers, and steamboat lines that covered most of the waters around New York. He had so many vessels in commission (well over twenty), most of which he had built himself, that the title of "Commodore" was bestowed upon him, at first facetiously but later in all seriousness, in recognition of his tremendous maritime power and accomplishments. In many respects he was the exact opposite of William Walker—whom he would eventually destroy. Vanderbilt was tall, virile (he sired thirteen children), physically powerful, loudmouthed and profane in his speech, highly successful in business, and a multimillionaire. He had quit school at the age of ten, but was endowed with extraordinary natural intelligence. When asked about the secret of his success, he replied: "I never tell anybody about what I'm going to do until after I've done it."

The outbreak of gold fever in California offered the Commodore another promising opportunity in the field of transportation. The Pacific Mail Steamship Company monopolized most of the travel business to California, running steamers to connect with both shores of Panama. The price was six hundred dollars for the round trip, New York to California, and the service was very poor.

"I can improve on that," asserted Vanderbilt. "I can make money at $300, crossing my passengers by Lake Nicaragua, a much shorter route."

The Commodore visited Nicaragua in 1849 and managed to obtain the exclusive right to construct an interoceanic canal. In the meantime, pending its construction, he acquired a right-of-way between the oceans in Nicaragua and a monopoly of navigation with steam vessels on Lake Nicaragua. His enterprise, to be known as the Accessory Transit Company, had a contract with the government of Nicaragua to transport passengers across the isthmus. Under its terms the Nicaraguan government was supposed to be paid ten thousand dollars per year, plus 10 percent of the transit company's profits, for this privilege. The Accessory Transit Company, however, owned only the river and lake steamers, the buildings, and various other facilities in Nicaragua. The ocean-going steamers were owned by a separate and privately owned Vanderbilt company. The Commodore could thus make annual accounting adjustments, described by his rivals as "juggling the books," to show that the Accessory Transit Company in Nicaragua constantly operated at a loss, while large profits were made by the ocean-going vessels outside the jurisdiction of Nicaragua. As a result, Vanderbilt habitually claimed that the transit company owed no taxes to the Nicaraguan government.

CORNELIUS VANDERBILT (1794–1877)

Financier, known as the Commodore, established the Accessory Transit Company between New York and California, via Nicaragua, in 1850. When William Walker, as president of Nicaragua, seized the lucrative transit company in 1856, Vanderbilt cut off the shipments of men and supplies he had been sending Walker and aided Costa Rica in defeating the arrogant filibuster.

On Vanderbilt's line, passengers from New York and New Orleans went by ship to Greytown (San Juan del Norte), a Nicaraguan port on the Atlantic side, then proceeded on shallow-draft riverboats up the navigable San Juan River about 120 miles to the small village of San Carlos on the eastern shore of Lake Nicaragua. Ferry-type steamers would transport them some fifty-six miles across the lake to Virgin Bay on the western side of Lake Nicaragua.

The final stage of the Nicaraguan transit was mostly by mule or on foot along the rough twelve-mile Transit Road from Virgin Bay to the Pacific port of San Juan del Sur. Large ocean-going vessels would then meet the travelers to take them up to San Francisco.

ACCIDENT ON PANAMA RAILROAD NEAR GATUN LAKE
The trip from the East Coast of the United States to California in the 1850s was hazardous by way of either Panama or Nicaragua.

VANDERBILT'S "STAR OF THE WEST," 1852

This wooden sidewheel steamship of three decks—1,172 tons—was
built in 1852 at a cost of $250,000. It was sold by Cornelius Vanderbilt
to the Accessory Transit Company for use on the Nicaragua route
between New York and San Juan del Norte from 1852 to 1856. During
the Civil War it was used by the Union army as a troop transport ship.
It was captured by the Confederates in 1862 and burned in New Orleans.

At first the Transit Road was a precarious gutter of mud and
rocks, where hikers and even mules would occasionally get
stuck in the quagmire. Gradually the roadway was improved
so much that a few lucky passengers could ride in wagons
hauled by oxen or horse-drawn carriages. Mark Twain made
this twelve-mile trip in 1866 in three and a half hours in a mule-
drawn, faded mud wagon, describing the Transit Road journey
as a "jolly little scamper across the Isthmus."

The most picturesque portion of this tiresome journey was
the stretch along the noble San Juan River, lined on each side
with virgin tropical forest. Passengers were awed by its majes-
tic beauty—the deep verdure of the luxuriant foliage, vigorous
vines, and brilliant varicolored flowers. The natural splendor
of the riverscape made most passengers overlook the tedious
inconveniences caused by the difficult struggle of the riverboats

up and through a seemingly never-ending series of rapids, where loose rocks, shallow water, and eventually a sandbar frequently caused the laboring steamers to run aground.

Vanderbilt usually charged about $300 for a first-class passage or $180 steerage for the trip from New York to San Francisco via Nicaragua. The fares of a rival transportation company passing though Panama were roughly twice as much (although there were frequent changes in the passenger rates). Vanderbilt's ships, however, were described by his rivals as "floating pig-sties."

The first trip of the Vanderbilt Steamship Line from New York to California in July and August 1851 took forty-five days: ten days on the Atlantic, twenty days passing through Nicaragua, and fifteen days on the Pacific. Shortly after his arrival in San Francisco one of the 110 passengers on the S. S. *Pacific* gave the following vivid account of the journey to a reporter of the San Francisco *Alta California:*

> The accommodations, or in fact the want of them on the steamer, beggars all description. I have been on the Pacific sea six times; never saw the like in my life, anywhere. . . . The potatoes gave out in three days; no fresh bread; the ship's biscuit was old, rotten and wormy, and was put in the oven every day to drive out and kill the insects; the fish stunk; the oranges instead of coming to the table, were sold at the bar for 12½ cents per piece; soda water at fifty cents a glass. . . . At Acapulco no beef was taken in, there being still some half-dead cows on board, whose natural end was only anticipated by the butcher a day or two. Eight dozen chickens were laid in there, and when within three days from this port, matters and things became so woeful that nothing but the fact of a passenger having three dozen chickens as freight on board, saved us from positive starvation.

A year later service on the Nicaragua route was much improved and passengers, enjoying reasonable comfort, were able to make the trip from New York to California in about twenty-five days. The Vanderbilt Steamship Line advertisement was revised to read "THROUGH AHEAD OF ANY OTHER LINE."

When London capitalists refused to help Cornelius Vanderbilt finance the construction of a canal through Nicaragua, the Commodore gave up the plan of building the canal and sold his steamships to the Accessory Transit Company. Between 1853

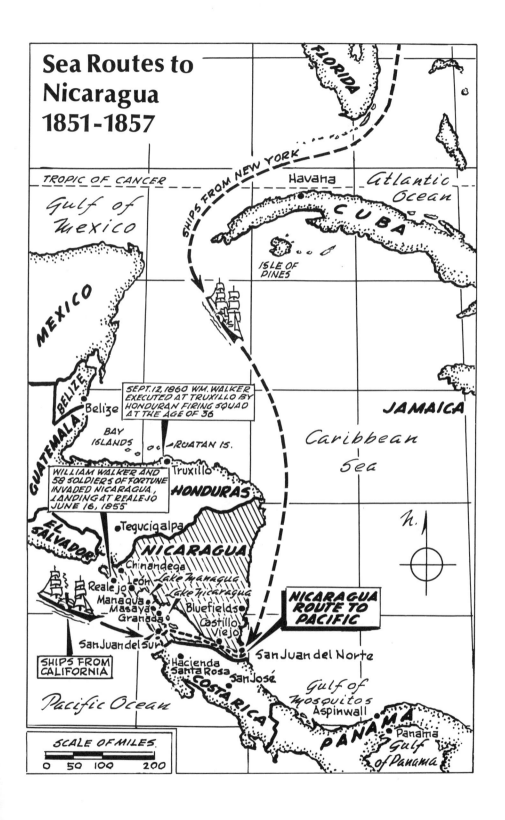

Sea Routes to Nicaragua 1851-1857

FLORIDA

SHIPS FROM NEW YORK

TROPIC OF CANCER

Gulf of Mexico

Havana

Atlantic Ocean

CUBA

ISLE OF PINES

MEXICO

BELIZE

GUATEMALA

Belize

BAY ISLANDS

ROATAN IS.

SEPT. 12, 1860 WM. WALKER EXECUTED AT TRUXILLO BY HONDURAN FIRING SQUAD AT THE AGE OF 36

JAMAICA

Caribbean Sea

Truxillo

WILLIAM WALKER AND 58 SOLDIERS OF FORTUNE INVADED NICARAGUA, LANDING AT REALEJO JUNE 16, 1855

HONDURAS

EL SALVADOR

Tegucigalpa

NICARAGUA

Chinandega

León

Lake Managua

Realejo

Managua

Lake Nicaragua

Masaya

Bluefields

Granada

NICARAGUA ROUTE TO PACIFIC

Castillo Viejo

San Juan del Sur

SHIPS FROM CALIFORNIA

Hacienda Santa Rosa

San Juan del Norte

San José

COSTA RICA

Gulf of Mosquitos

Pacific Ocean

Aspinwall

PANAMA

Panama

Gulf of Panama

SCALE OF MILES.

0   50   100   200

THE NIGGER EMPEROR OF NICARAGUA ON HIS THRONE.

ANONYMOUS 1839 CARTOON REFERS TO THE VAST QUANTITIES OF RUM AND IMPERIALIST SUPPORT GIVEN BY FREDERICK CHATFIELD, THE BRITISH CONSUL IN CENTRAL AMERICA, TO THE "MOSQUITO KING" OR "NIGGER EMPEROR" OF NICARAGUA—A PUPPET OF ENGLAND WHO RULED OVER A SWAMPY BRITISH PROTECTORATE ON THE COAST OF EASTERN NICARAGUA TO THE DETRIMENT OF THE NICARAGUANS

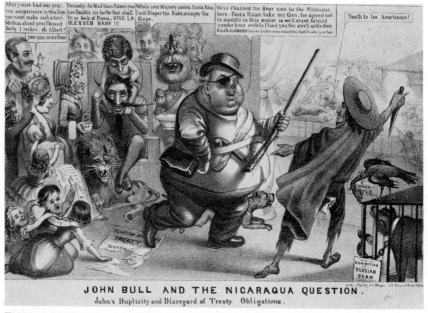

JOHN BULL AND THE NICARAGUA QUESTION.
John's Duplicity and Disregard of Treaty Obligations.

THIS POLITICAL CARTOON CHIDES GREAT BRITAIN FOR MEDDLING AND DOUBLE-DEALING IN CENTRAL AMERICAN POLITICS DURING THE 1850s

VIEW OF THE PROPOSED NICARAGUA CANAL
THAT WAS NEVER COMPLETED

THE NAVIGABLE SAN JUAN RIVER WAS A VITAL 120-MILE LINK
IN THE NICARAGUA ROUTE BETWEEN NEW YORK AND CALIFORNIA
IN THE 1850s

"UNCLE SAM" IS FACED BY THE
PROBLEM OF A CANAL IN
NICARAGUA OR PANAMA

and 1856 two other North American financiers, Charles Morgan
and C. K. Garrison, feuded constantly with Vanderbilt over
control of this transit company.

It had not been easy for Vanderbilt to develop this lucrative
transit business, which transported over 100,000 passengers
through Nicaragua between 1851 and 1857. In the 1840s the
British government had actively challenged the expanding
American interests in Central America. Great Britain had
already established a colony in Belize (British Honduras),
claimed the Bay Islands near Belize, and many years previously
created the protectorate known as the Mosquito Kingdom—a
low-lying, swampy region along the coast of eastern Nicaragua
about three hundred miles long and forty miles wide, extending
from Cape Honduras to the San Juan River. To forestall the
construction of a proposed canal across Nicaragua, in 1847
Frederick Chatfield, the British consul in Central America,
informed the Nicaraguan government that the proposed canal's
eastern terminus, the mouth of the San Juan River, would lie
within the Mosquito Kingdom and therefore would come under

British jurisdiction. Instigated by Britain, the Mosquito king notified Nicaragua that it had until January 1, 1848, to withdraw from the port of San Juan del Norte. When the Nicaraguans protested, British marines landed, drove out the Nicaraguan officials, raised the Mosquito flag, and rechristened the port Greytown. The British then extended the southern boundary of the Mosquito Kingdom by twelve miles, officially shutting off Nicaragua from both banks of the proposed Nicaraguan canal.

Britain took very good care of the Mosquito king, according to a New York newspaper:

> His Mosquito Majesty, with all his court, consisting of a pet monkey, two parrots and a jug of rum . . . was allowed to get royally drunk three times a day . . . whilst wrapped in the folds of the British flag and fanned to sleep by the amiable paw of the British Lion.

In 1849 Ephraim George Squier, an archaeologist newly named as the American chargé d'affaires in Central America, was instructed by Secretary of State John M. Clayton to use all moral means to frustrate the designs of Great Britain in the Mosquito Kingdom and along the San Juan River; Squier was to assist the American capitalist Vanderbilt and his associates in obtaining from Nicaragua the right of transit for the proposed canal, but was to avoid an American monopoly and seek only an equal passage right for all nations through the proposed canal.

NICARAGUAN POSTAGE STAMP One of William Walker's unrealized plans was to make Nicaragua the main highway for commerce between the Atlantic and Pacific oceans. Many years after his death this Nicaraguan postage stamp, depicting the menacing volcano Momotombo in eruption, was successfully used as documentary evidence by backers of Panama to show how dangerous it would be to construct a trans-isthmian canal in Nicaragua. The United States Congress was duly impressed; in 1902 Panama, rather than Nicaragua, was selected as the site for the canal.

With Squier's assistance Vanderbilt and his group obtained the concession from the government of Nicaragua, but there was still the threat that the British fleet might block the entrance to the San Juan River near Greytown. Secretary Clayton met with the British agent in Washington, Sir Henry Bulwer, and the resulting Clayton-Bulwer Treaty of 1850 served as a compromise solution to the existing Anglo-American problems. The treaty ruled out American and British colonization in Central America, prohibited both the United States and Britain from exercising exclusive control over the proposed canal, and provided for United States–British cooperation in the construction of such a canal. This enabled Vanderbilt to proceed with the activities of the Accessory Transit Company in Nicaragua. Although the treaty made Greytown a free city, it was still virtually under the control of the British consul, and for several years there was constant friction between the British official and the transit company.

TYPICAL NICARAGUAN TRANSPORTATION DURING THE 1850s

7

The Lure of Nicaragua

By the middle of 1854 William Walker had become a respected hero in California and was chosen as a delegate to the state Democratic convention in Sacramento. The petty intrigues of local California politics disgusted him, however, and he welcomed the opportunity to return to newspaper work. He was employed for several months as an editor of the Sacramento *Democratic State Journal*; he then moved back to San Francisco as editor of the San Francisco *Commercial Advertiser*, a position offered to him by its publisher, Byron Cole.

Cole was a New Englander who had developed a keen interest in Central America—especially Nicaragua. He managed to convince Walker to forget Sonora and give his unreserved support to the American colonization of Nicaragua, where success seemed far more likely. Cole himself had made the trip from the East to San Francisco, not across the vast expanse of unoccupied and sometimes hostile plains between the eastern states and the Pacific, or by way of unhealthy Panama, but via Nicaragua on the Vanderbilt Steamship Line.

In his trip through Nicaragua, Cole had been much impressed by the luxuriant tropical vegetation, warm, pleasant climate, and strategic geographical position of that country—it seemed ideal for a future passageway between Europe and the Orient. This was indeed fertile territory for Manifest Destiny and a worthy challenge to ambitious filibusters.

Nicaragua was in the throes of political turmoil. Since acquiring independence from Spain in 1821, following some three hundred years of Spanish colonial rule, this picturesque Central American country had constantly been beset by political upheaval and revolution. Between 1847 and 1855 there were no less than thirteen leaders of the Nicaraguan government, known as "supreme directors." Fruto Chamorro, a Legitimist (Conservative), was elected supreme director in 1853, but managed to have the Constitution changed in 1854 to give the supreme director the title of president, vastly increase his powers, and lengthen the term of office from two years to four. This high-handed move was violently opposed by the other major political party in Nicaragua, known as the Democratic or Liberal opposition, led by Francisco Castellón. Chamorro claimed that Castellón was trying to launch a treasonous uprising, and exiled him. Following the normal pattern of the time in Nicaragua, Castellón did indeed start a revolution against Chamorro.

With so much political instability, it seemed to Cole and Walker that Nicaragua needed a violent change in order to bring about law, order, and progress. The young republic was rich in natural resources: valuable tropical hardwoods; abundant minerals, including gold and copper; plantations of anil (indigo dye), sugar, cotton, corn, and tropical fruits; and extensive haciendas of cattle. Economically, however, the country was in ruin. Agricultural laborers were unavailable, since most had to serve in either the Legitimist or Democratic armies. The population, estimated at 250,000, had been ravaged by disease, poverty, and constant revolution. Women outnumbered men three to two. About 50 percent of the people were of mixed Spanish-Indian blood, one-third were pure Indian, about one-tenth were white, and the remaining 7 percent were Negroes. Owing to the constant civil war there was little education.

The two main political parties were constantly struggling for power in Nicaragua. The Legitimists, who dominated the southern half of the republic and maintained their stronghold in Granada, had closer ties with Great Britain and Europe, were more conservative, and were more closely bound to the Catholic Church; the opposing Democrats, who controlled northern Nicaragua and had their seat of government in León, were more liberal, both in their religious outlook and with regard to freedom of the press. Throughout Central America the pro-British Conservatives generally represented the church and the wealthy, while the Liberals were more anticlerical, more

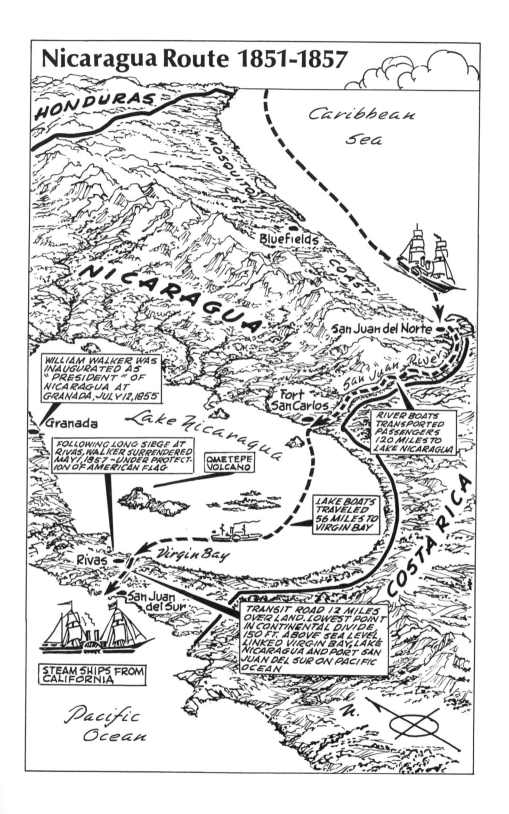

Nicaragua Route 1851-1857

HONDURAS

Caribbean Sea

MOSQUITO COAST

Bluefields

NICARAGUA

San Juan del Norte

San Juan River

WILLIAM WALKER WAS INAUGURATED AS "PRESIDENT" OF NICARAGUA AT GRANADA, JULY 12, 1855

Granada

Lake Nicaragua

Fort San Carlos

RIVER BOATS TRANSPORTED PASSENGERS 120 MILES TO LAKE NICARAGUA

FOLLOWING LONG SIEGE AT RIVAS, WALKER SURRENDERED MAY 1, 1857 — UNDER PROTECTION OF AMERICAN FLAG

OMETEPE VOLCANO

LAKE BOATS TRAVELED 56 MILES TO VIRGIN BAY

COSTA RICA

Rivas

Virgin Bay

San Juan del Sur

TRANSIT ROAD 12 MILES OVERLAND. LOWEST POINT IN CONTINENTAL DIVIDE, 150 FT. ABOVE SEA LEVEL, LINKED VIRGIN BAY, LAKE NICARAGUA AND PORT SAN JUAN DEL SUR ON PACIFIC OCEAN

STEAM SHIPS FROM CALIFORNIA

Pacific Ocean

N.

favorably inclined toward the United States, and somewhat more benevolent to the underprivileged.

It was really not a class struggle, however, for in Nicaragua there were a few rich families and many poor and shoeless in each party. Granada depended heavily on agriculture, León more on commerce and trade. The hostility between the two factions was mainly regional rather than ideological.

Cole's description of the political turmoil in Nicaragua exerted a considerable influence on Walker. In Cole's opinion the British were supporting the Legitimists or Conservatives throughout Central America in order to promote Britain's eventual domination of the whole region. In the United States the administration of President Franklin Pierce seemed to be confused by Central American politics, although they *were* interested in the transit route and the possibility of a canal through Nicaragua.

Cole and Walker became convinced that, despite U. S. neutrality laws, the Democrats of Nicaragua should be supported— partly to thwart the British, but mostly because in their opinion Nicaragua deserved to be Americanized by the importation of American institutions and Anglo-Saxon settlers. Perhaps a determined group of privately organized American soldiers of fortune who supported the Democratic cause could "save" Nicaragua. Walker idealistically (but erroneously) believed that he could eventually regenerate all of Central America, starting with Nicaragua; perhaps he could accomplish for Nicaragua what Byron had tried to do for Greece.

Cole made two trips to Nicaragua in 1854 and finally returned to California with a contract formally granting substantial tracts of Nicaraguan land and permission to colonize this land. (At Walker's insistence, no mention was made of military intervention so as to avoid problems with United States neutrality laws—difficulties that had frustrated him in the Sonora expedition.) Francisco Castellón, representing the Liberal party in Nicaragua ("the outs") promised three hundred colonists the right to cultivate land and granted them in perpetuity the privilege of bearing arms. Castellón expected these three hundred colonists to be mere mercenary soldiers who would help him to oust the Legitimist government of his hated rival, President Fruto Chamorro, who represented "the ins." Any benefits for the colonists, of course, were contingent upon an ultimate victory by the Nicaraguan Liberal party following a revolution.

In February 1855 Walker gave up his newspaper work and devoted himself completely to organizing his second filibustering expedition. This time, unlike what occurred during the Sonora debacle, the United States authorities in California gave Walker their tacit approval. Major General John E. Wool, commanding the Pacific Division, went even further—he shook Walker heartily by the hand and stated that he not only would not interfere with the Nicaraguan colonization enterprise, but wished it complete success.

Legal difficulties having been overcome, Walker's most pressing problem was financial. His own resources were scanty, and considerable sums would be needed to finance the filibustering expedition to Nicaragua. An unseaworthy, leaky brig named the *Vesta* was chartered, and the bare minimum of food, arms, and military supplies were obtained.

Between February and May 1855 Walker had to solicit, beg, and plead for funds to finance the forthcoming enterprise. A few dollars here, a few dollars there were raised, but the money collected was insufficient to pay for adequate provisions and troops.

In the midst of this fund raising, on March 12, 1855, the irrepressible Walker became involved in another pistol duel, cause unknown, with a crack shot named William Carter. Again Walker missed his antagonist, but Carter's first bullet hit the Filibuster on the foot, ending the contest.

REPUBLIC OF NICARAGUA,
DEPARTMENT OF COLONIZATION,

It is hereby certified that, under the Decree of the Supreme Government of Nicaragua relative to Colonization, dated November 23d, 1855, *Samuel Carpenter,*

man of family - having declared before me his intention of settling in Nicaragua, according to the provisions of said Decree, is permitted to select and occupy a Square Section of *Three* HUNDRED AND FIFTY ACRES OF LAND, from the Public Land *in the Depart ment of Rivas*

Alternate Sections are reserved for Government.

No Locations can be made within a mile and a half of the populated limits of any town or city.

Immediate notice of occupancy, with description of the land occupied, must be forwarded to this Department.

Given under my hand and the Seal of the Department, at Granada, this *28th* day of *March, 1856.*

MANY UNITED STATES CITIZENS WENT TO NICARAGUA AS COLONIZERS AND ACTUALLY RECEIVED CONCESSIONS FROM WALKER'S ARMY TO SELECT AND OCCUPY 350 ACRES OF NICARAGUAN LAND

8

The Fifty-eight "Immortals"

FINALLY fifty-eight soldiers of fortune boarded the *Vesta* at San Francisco. Some were experienced veterans; others included disappointed and luckless miners and prospectors, drifters, wharf bums, and ne'er-do-wells. These fifty-eight men were to be known as "William Walker's Immortals." Among them were some exceptionally able officers: C. C. Hornsby and Frank Anderson, both of whom had served with distinction in the United States Army during the Mexican War; Achilles Kewan, who had fought with Narciso López in his ill-fated attempt to liberate Cuba; and Timothy Crocker, who had loyally accompanied Walker through all the miseries of the campaign in Sonora.

As in the case of the disastrous Sonora expedition, Walker, the knight-errant, had to embark on a foreign military adventure surreptitiously—but for a very different reason. The provisions for the voyage had been bought on credit; when the merchants demanded payment, Walker, now virtually penniless, was unable to pay. Thereupon the sheriff of San Francisco boarded the *Vesta* and ordered it attached for debt. A deputy sheriff named Purdy was left on board to spend the night to make sure the brig would not leave port.

At midnight Walker invited Purdy to join him for a drink in the cabin. The unsuspecting official complied. As *Harper's Weekly* later reported, when the door was shut, Walker, in a slow, quiet Tennessee drawl, calmly informed the deputy sheriff that he was a prisoner: "There, sir, are cigars and champagne; and there are handcuffs and irons. Pray, take your choice."

The deputy sheriff, a practical man, decided to settle for the champagne and was in a cheerful frame of mind several hours later when he was put on board the steam tug that had, in the meantime, towed the *Vesta* to a point well outside the harbor.

As Purdy returned to port, presumably to answer some awkward questions from his superiors, the *Vesta* spread her sails and stood out to sea, passing through the Golden Gate en route to Nicaragua early on the morning of May 4, 1855.

Since there was no formal crew, owing to lack of funds, the *Vesta* was worked by men detailed from the passengers. Walker, still bothered by his duel-wounded foot, limped restlessly around the deck, attempting to maintain order and discipline.

On June 16 the *Vesta* reached Realejo, a Pacific port of Nicaragua now known as Corinto. The fifty-eight Immortals leaped ashore for the first time in the deceptively beautiful and bountiful land where many were to perish.

PORT OF REALEJO, NICARAGUA
On June 16, 1855, William Walker landed at Realejo, a Pacific port of Nicaragua, with fifty-eight soldiers of fortune; a year later Walker became president of Nicaragua.

The slovenly-appearing soldiers of the Nicaraguan Democratic party, small in stature and armed with antiquated muskets, were wearing only tattered rags as uniforms when they greeted their arrogant new comrades from the North. The taller, more powerful, bearded filibusters, equipped with rifles, revolvers, and bowie knives, observed them with amusement and contempt. The bare feet of the ill-nourished Nicaraguans contrasted with the sturdy miners' boots of the aggressive visitors, most of whom wore red or blue flannel shirts, blue cotton britches, and wide-brimmed black felt hats, usually cocked at a devil-may-care angle.

The native population received the bearded Yanqui strangers cordially. After six long weeks at sea the Americans were restless and eager to let off some steam at the local *pulperías* of Realejo, where there was plenty of cheap aguardiente, a powerful colorless rum made from sugarcane. Some comely, flirtatious señoritas were also in evidence, standing about and forming a pleasing contrast to the drab, shabby thatched huts and mud-plastered walls. Walker warned his troops, however, that anyone caught molesting a lady, looting, or desecrating the local church would be immediately executed by a firing squad.

The following morning the filibusters proceeded inland to the revolutionary Democratic capital of León, where they were welcomed by a cheering throng. En route they got their first close look at beautiful Nicaragua. The rainy season had just started, and verdant splendor was everywhere to be seen: vigorous tropical vegetation, fences of green cactus, coconut palms, silk-cotton and mango trees, bamboos, banana plants, blossoming purple morning glories, and brilliant scarlet bougainvilleas. Lizards of various colors and sizes were basking in the sunshine. Gorgeous exotic Central American birds could be seen and heard on all sides, not to mention chattering parrots and monkeys. It seemed to Walker that nature had done much for the country but man little.

The stinking poverty of the local villages through which they passed—brought on by countless revolutions—contrasted with the natural splendor of the rural areas. León itself was an at-

VOLCANO OF OMETEPE, VIRGIN BAY, LAKE NICARAGUA
Virgin Bay was an integral part of Vanderbilt's transit route through Nicaragua. The Transit Road started here, a distance of only twelve miles from the Nicaraguan port on the Pacific known as San Juan del Sur.

tractive city of some twenty thousand inhabitants, with many rows of tile-covered formal adobe houses. There were several Spanish-type plazas surrounded by imposing public buildings and churches, some of them bullet-scarred. The noble cathedral of Saint Peter was of Spanish-Moorish architecture. The towering volcanoes Viejo and Momotombo formed an imposing background.

MARKETPLACE ON THE GRAND PLAZA, MANAGUA, NICARAGUA
Nicaragua, disturbed by constant political unrest, appealed to William
Walker, who believed all Central America should become a vast slave
empire dominated by the Anglo-Saxon race.

Francisco Castellón, the defeated political leader of the Nicaraguan Democrats who had offered the Americans their "colonization" grant, was especially glad to see Walker, since his own
fortunes had been declining at an alarming rate. Even though
Fruto Chamorro, the Legitimist strong man, had recently died,
the military power of the Conservative opposition seemed to
be increasing in a most menacing manner. A contingent of one
thousand Legitimist troops was being organized near Managua
under General Ponciano Corral; to make matters worse, Legitimist conscription of soldiers was being effectively pushed in
other areas of Nicaragua controlled by the Conservatives.
Castellón felt threatened on all sides. Walker was given the
rank of colonel, while his troops were to be called *La Falange
Americana*, the American Phalanx. Walker and his men immediately became naturalized Nicaraguan citizens, since a simple declaration of intent was the only requirement.

In point of fact, the Filibuster was delighted that things were
going so badly for Castellón's party: the worse off the Democrats were, the more urgently they would need him, and the
better his chances would be to dominate and Americanize
Nicaragua.

Castellón was a timid, vacillating personality; his commander
in chief, the haughty and pompous General José Trinidad
Muñoz, as well as his sullen aide, Colonel Félix Ramirez, re-

sented the presence of the Americans and both were openly contemptuous of Walker. When Walker and General Muñoz met for the first time they took an instant dislike to each other, arguing about military history and strategy. In contrast to the quiet, skinny Walker, the loud and flamboyant Muñoz was so fat he seemed to be bursting out of his elaborate gold-braided red and blue uniform.

Walker's first military plan of action was to gain control of the Transit Road, to take it by force from the opposing Legitimist troops in order to acquire additional recruits from among the passengers crossing the isthmus, from both California and the East. A voyage of four days down the coast was necessary so that the strategic town of Rivas, near the Transit Road, could be attacked by surprise.

HALFWAY HOUSE ON THE TRANSIT ROAD FROM LAKE NICARAGUA TO SAN JUAN DEL SUR, THE PORT ON THE PACIFIC OCEAN

Walker's 58 filibusters and some 110 Nicaraguan troops under Colonel Ramirez boarded the *Vesta*. A volunteer revolutionary named Mariano Mendez spread his blanket on the deck and organized a card game called monte, which lasted the entire trip. The unscrupulous Mendez managed to win all the loose cash the poor, naive native soldiers had with them. Mendez, a pure Indian with a violent, uncontrollable temper, had been through countless revolutions. At first he was loyal to Walker—in fact, he wouldn't take any orders at all from his Nicaraguan superior officer, Colonel Ramirez, whom he characterized as a "dog." Ramirez sulked in a corner of the deck, angry at Mendez and jealous of Walker. In a confidential chat during a break in

CHINANDEGA, NICARAGUA

the card game Mendez admonished Walker that the only way to get ahead in Nicaragua was with a whip in one hand and silver in the other.

The troops landed at night and were soon drenched by a heavy tropical downpour as they tramped along unfamiliar trails in the dense rain forest, ankle-deep in mud. At daylight the two groups breakfasted separately: the Americans on hardtack and cold meat, the natives on frijoles and tortillas. Following a siesta, the advance continued through the dark, moist forest. By nightfall the attackers reached the village of Tola, where, following a brief skirmish, they routed a small Legitimist garrison and obtained shelter for the night. Several enemy soldiers were wounded and captured. Mariano Mendez was about to bayonet these unfortunates, but Walker stopped him and ordered the American surgeon to bind up their wounds. Mendez was indignant and deeply offended.

The next morning the company marched along the road in the direction of Rivas. The skies had cleared; the atmosphere was soft, balmy, and delightful. Just as if they had been friendly tourists, the Americans were greeted along the way with smiles from market women with baskets on their heads. As the weary, sweating men reached the summit of a hill they were rewarded by a breathtaking view, in full sunlight, of Lake Nicaragua, with the tall, graceful cone of the volcano Concepción rising from its bluish depths. In the distance, deceptively peaceful, the church towers of Rivas were to be seen. Their pleasure in this idyllic landscape was short-lived; Walker abruptly ordered them to move on and prepare for the attack.

On June 29, 1855, the battle of Rivas commenced on a thickly wooded plain on the outskirts of the town. It was evident that the Legitimists had been forewarned about the arrival of the filibusters, for a number of wooden barricades had been hastily erected. Walker's usual plan of attack was to drive straight for the main plaza in the center of a town and strike at the heart of the enemy. The filibusters charged into Rivas with loud yells, and the battle was on.

When the first shots were fired, the native troops under

Ramirez broke ranks and fled into the woods, leaving the Americans to fight alone. Their first frontal assault was repulsed with disastrous results for Walker: he lost two of his most capable officers, Lieutenant Colonel Achilles Kewan and Major Timothy Crocker, as well as thirteen other Americans. The narrow, muddy streets of Rivas, lined with squalid adobe houses, were tenaciously defended by the Legitimists, who outnumbered the vulnerable filibusters eight to one. Walker himself, in a third-person account written in later years, gave a vivid description of young Crocker's heroic last effort in the battle of Rivas:

> Walker rode past just as the houses were entered; and seeing Crocker a short distance in advance, he called out to know how far the men had got toward the Plaza. Crocker was panting with excitement; his chin was bleeding from the graze of a bullet, one arm hung useless, being shot through near the shoulder, while in the hand of the other side he carried his army revolver, with half its barrels discharged. But the rage of battle was on him; and heedless of wounds he was trying to drive the men toward the enemy. As soon, however, as he saw his commander, he sank his voice, and said in a low tone, "Colonel, the men falter; I cannot get them on."

A moment later the gallant Crocker was shot dead, an irreplaceable loss for the American Phalanx. The Legitimists poured in from all sides, as the Americans took cover wherever they could. After several hours of violent door-to-door fighting, during which the filibusters tried in vain to seize the main plaza, Walker ordered a retreat, leaving behind half a dozen wounded. The battle had been furious—it was reported that the enemy losses were roughly ten times as great as the Americans'. In all fairness it should be noted that the long Yankee rifles and up-to-date Colt revolvers were more effective weapons than the antiquated muskets of the Legitimists.

Having gotten off to a bad start, Walker trudged back to the Transit Road and retreated to the Pacific port of San Juan del Sur with his exhausted, forlorn, defeated troops. Impressing into service a Costa Rican schooner that happened to be in the harbor, the surviving gringos climbed aboard to lick their wounds and return to Realejo and León—with the utmost haste, since the enemy was in hot pursuit.

Their flight was marred by one ominous incident. Near the beach at San Juan del Sur a dissolute gambler from California named Dewey, accompanied by a local fisherman known as Sam, set fire to some buildings in the town in the erroneous belief that this might help the filibusters, hurt the Legitimists, and in any event enable them to do some looting on the side during the excitement caused by the conflagration. Walker, who disapproved of vandalism, was very much incensed by this wanton act. By now night was closing in and there was no time to be lost: the enemy was already approaching the beach. Walker hastily summoned a court-martial, which condemned

PORT OF SAN JUAN DEL SUR ON THE PACIFIC OCEAN, NICARAGUA

Dewey and Sam to be executed. During the confusion—there was already scattered firing from the advance guard of the enemy—Sam managed to slip the ropes binding his wrists and escape. The drunken Dewey, accompanied by Sam's native mistress, tried to seek safety in a small fishing boat—but to no avail, for this small boat was soon caught and made fast to the schooner, which left port by the ebb tide and headed for the open sea.

"THE IMMIGRANT"

"Go to the tropics, boy, the glorious tropics, where the sun is supreme, and never shares its dominion with blue-nosed, leaden-colored, rheumy-eyed frost-gods; go there, and catch the matchless tints of the skies, the living emerald of the forests, and the light-giving azure of the waters; go where the birds are rainbow-hued, and the very fish are golden." From "Waikna," by Samuel A. Bard (pseudonym of Ephraim George Squier).

The following morning Walker ordered Dewey, who was being towed behind the schooner in the fishing smack, to come aboard the schooner to stand trial. Dewey, armed with two revolvers and shielded by Sam's mistress, told the filibuster to go to hell in no uncertain terms. The shooting started, and a few minutes later Dewey was dead. The native woman was wounded in the thigh, an injury that was soon treated by Walker's surgeon.

This incident is only one example of Walker's absolute ruthlessness in punishing plunderers. The diminutive leader possessed some unusual inherent power or voice of command that enabled him to mold together and demand complete obedience from a motley group, many of whom were rebellious roughnecks and lawless adventurers. But to defy him invited death.

It had been a hectic baptism of fire for the filibusters. When they got back to León they were sickened to learn that the six wounded comrades they had been forced to leave behind at Rivas had been chained to a pile of fagots in the town plaza and burned alive.

WALKER AND HIS ARMY ON BOARD A STEAMER NEAR
VIRGIN BAY, NICARAGUA

9

Political and Military Intrigue

I N JULY 1855 the publisher Byron Cole joined Walker, bringing with him a former Prussian cavalry officer, Bruno von Natzmer, whose knowledge of Spanish and familiarity with the Nicaraguan terrain would be helpful to the filibusters.

Cole obtained for Walker a new grant from Castellón, authorizing the recruitment of three hundred additional men for military service in Nicaragua. They were to be paid one hundred dollars per month and promised five hundred acres of land as a bonus when the fighting was over. It was no longer necessary to maintain the fiction of colonization, since Walker was now safely beyond the jurisdiction of United States neutrality laws.

Cole also persuaded Castellón to authorize Walker to adjust the problems and differences that existed between Nicaragua and Vanderbilt's Accessory Transit Company concerning the transit route (a temporary adjustment, as it turned out).

By this time it was gradually becoming clear that Walker had not come to Nicaragua with mercenary soldiers merely to further the revolutionary designs of a frustrated politician and help him gain the presidency of the republic. Walker was no paid Hessian, and he certainly did not intend to fight simply for Castellón's cause. The commander in chief of the American Phalanx wanted much more: he hoped to Americanize Nicaragua.

William Walker was a believer in the survival of the fittest. He came to Nicaragua to "regenerate" the country under Anglo-

Saxon control. Like Adolf Hitler some eighty years later, he believed implicitly in the inherent superiority of the blond, blue-eyed Anglo-Saxon over the dark hybrid race of Indian, Negro, and Spanish heritage he found in Nicaragua. If Walker had been successful he would have instituted a revived form of African slavery as the cornerstone of his imperialistic system, under which not only African Negroes (to be imported in due course), but also local Central American laborers were to be the slaves or serfs. He could not foresee that within ten years slavery would be abolished in the United States.

Walker first came to Nicaragua with missionary zeal, wishing to bring a revival to the country and make it a territory friendly to the southern United States, a land that would be traversed by a canal uniting the Atlantic and Pacific oceans. As time passed this limited goal became more grandiose. Eventually the Filibuster envisaged a great Central American Anglo-Saxon Empire, with himself as its leader, whose agricultural and mineral wealth would be developed through slavery and whose economy would be bolstered by international dependence on a Nicaraguan canal. The proud heritage of Spanish-American culture meant little to William Walker.

Divergent goals inevitably led to quarrels and misunderstandings between Walker and the Nicaraguan Democrats. The Democratic leaders in Nicaragua, for example, didn't care much about controlling the Transit Road—which to Walker was all-important for keeping in touch with the outside world, enlisting new recruits, and receiving needed supplies. The Democrats, being "the outs," were content to stay on the defensive and just wanted to get back in power so that Castellón could become the undisputed president of Nicaragua. The aggressive Walker, on the other hand, was anxious to attack the enemy.

Walker had been incensed by the defection of his native allies at Rivas. He accused General Muñoz of treason, of giving orders to the native Nicaraguan troops not to fight but to run away. Upon their return to León there was a critical confrontation between Castellón, Muñoz, and Walker. The Legitimist enemy, under the command of General Corral and his Honduran ally, the dreaded General Santos Guardiola, was approaching León. To make matters worse, cholera had broken out in several Nicaraguan villages.

Walker temporarily withdrew his troops to the nearby town of Chinandega, meanwhile managing to obtain the services of some additional Nicaraguan soldiers to support him under the command of a retired colonel, José "Chelón" Valle—a jovial, robust Indian.

When General Muñoz was killed in battle near León, Walker at once became more vital to the Democratic cause. He decided to occupy Virgin Bay, the Accessory Transit Company harbor on Lake Nicaragua. His army, consisting of 50 Americans and 120 native soldiers under Valle, was attacked on September 3, 1855, by six hundred men under General Santos Guardiola—the "butcher of Honduras"—who vowed he would drive the gringo *falanginos* back into the lake.

Santos Guardiola was not a man to be trifled with: he did not take enemy prisoners—he earned his sanguinary nickname by burning them or bayoneting them. At the sound of his name women were said to have shuddered, crossed themselves, and uttered an Ave, while brave men felt for their knives or looked for the nearest exit.

Frank Leslie's Illustrated Newspaper described Santos Guardiola as a corpulent, dark-skinned man, with long, straight black hair, a low retreating forehead, and beetling eyebrows that shaded his glittering black eyes. His coarse, brutal features were supposed to have reflected his fiendish temper.

Many tales of the savage atrocities of this Honduran general were circulated throughout Central America. On one occasion, *Leslie's* reported, it was whispered that a common soldier in Guardiola's force who was posted as a guard on a river bank saw a young girl struggling in the rapids. Forgetting military discipline, he threw down his musket, jumped in, and rescued her from a watery grave. Hearing of this incident, the fierce general—whether from a desire to enforce rigid martial obedience or because of the impulses of a bloodthirsty disposition—condemned the unfortunate recruit to be shot at sundown.

GENERAL SANTOS GUARDIOLA, KNOWN TO WALKER'S TROOPS AS
THE "BUTCHER OF HONDURAS"

Following the execution, according to *Leslie's*, Guardiola in a fit of ill temper denied the body a Christian burial and ordered it to be tossed into the river.

Another story about Guardiola described an incident during a long forced march, when one of his soldiers collapsed on the ground from exhaustion. The general ordered him to get up immediately and keep on marching; the wretched man murmured that he was just too tired. "The Butcher" thereupon shot him on the spot—then turned to the other bedraggled recruits and asked "who else was tired."

Faced by such a formidable antagonist at Virgin Bay, with the lake behind them and no retreat possible, Walker and his troops had to fight or die. The Filibuster, although wounded slightly in the throat, exposed himself repeatedly to enemy fire as he rallied his followers to an unexpected victory. Sixty of the Legitimist enemy were killed, with virtually no losses to Walker's men.

Again the Nicaraguans were puzzled, as they had been at Tola, because Walker insisted upon caring for the enemy wounded as well as for his own wounded, instead of giving them the coup de grace, as was usual in Central America when dealing with captured foes.

Virgin Bay was a turning point for William Walker. The victory was enthusiastically acclaimed in newspapers throughout the United States. Nicaragua, on the other hand, was deeply disturbed, not only by Walker's military success but by the sudden death of Francisco Castellón at León, from cholera. The country desperately needed new leadership.

Additional American recruits had arrived on a transit vessel from San Francisco, under the command of the veteran filibuster Colonel Charles Gilman from Baltimore, who had been with Walker in Sonora and had lost a leg there. Walker's army now numbered about 250, all volunteers.

It was the custom in Nicaragua for both the Legitimists and Democrats to draft most available young peons (those they could catch) for forced military service. In the army, on either side, these wretched common soldiers were abused and bullied

WALKER'S TROOPS LANDING AT VIRGIN BAY, NICARAGUA

by ruthless native officers and sergeants. Walker decided he did not want impressed Nicaraguans in his army—only volunteers. The result was that he had very few native soldiers.

The ordinary Nicaraguan, although he may have instinctively disliked and feared the gringos, was even more afraid of the recruiting sergeants of his own country. Because of this benevolent policy, Walker himself, at least during the first few months he was in Nicaragua, gained a certain amount of sympathy among the impoverished and underprivileged. One incident gives dramatic testimony as to how some natives felt about

Walker. A prisoner of the Legitimists in Granada was offered his freedom and a reward of two thousand pesos to go to Walker's headquarters and murder him. Instead of killing the Filibuster, however, this clandestine agent informed him that the Legitimist capital of Granada was vulnerable, most of the defending troops having been moved to Rivas.

In mid-October 1855, in the most brilliant military maneuver of his career, Walker boldly attacked the Legitimist capital, Granada. On the evening of October 11 he seized the Accessory Transit Company's lake steamer, *La Virgen*, at Virgin Bay. The company's agent, Cortlandt Cushing, and the vessel's captain, Joseph N. Scott, protested in vain, claiming that the transit company's ship was American property under the protection of the American flag. Walker replied they were wrong: as a representative of the Nicaraguan government he had the perfect right to seize *La Virgen* for emergency use, since the steamer operated under the Nicaraguan flag in Nicaraguan waters.

The filibuster guard around the village of Virgin Bay was doubled so no one could leave under any pretext. The Legitimists at Granada were thus kept in ignorance of the impending danger.

Virgin Bay lies some forty miles distant from Granada on Lake Nicaragua. Under cover of darkness it took just a few hours for *La Virgen* to creep silently along the shore, carrying some 100 Americans and 250 native Democratic troops. All lights on board were extinguished. A very quiet landing was made on the lake shore some three miles north of Granada.

The troops stumbled about in total darkness in the luxuriant tropical vegetation growing near the shore. They quietly formed a long column with the Americans in the lead, the natives at the rear. At the first glimmer of dawn a local guide directed them to a main road leading into Granada.

As the filibusters reached the outskirts of the city, the church bells began to peal furiously. It was not a military alert, however, just a patriotic celebration. With the gaunt Colonel Hornsby leading the attack, the filibusters stormed the main plaza of Granada and quickly won the day. The Legitimist soldiers, caught off guard, were completely routed. A few sporadic shots were fired; two Legitimists and a Democratic drummer boy were killed. The Legitimists surrendered unconditionally to Walker.

Instead of a mere adventurer, William Walker had now become the most powerful political figure in Nicaragua, controlling both León and Granada.

GENERAL WALKER'S ENTRANCE INTO GRANADA, NICARAGUA

His first military order in Granada was a strict warning to his troops prohibiting looting, pillaging, and rape. This iron discipline was especially resented by his Democratic Nicaraguan followers, who had suffered painful losses of family and property from Legitimist actions in previous revolutions—and now thirsted for retaliation and revenge. Walker set free some one hundred political prisoners from the jails of Granada, many of whom had been languishing in chains.

The next day Walker received a delegation of Nicaraguan citizens who wished to declare him the provisional president of Nicaragua. The Filibuster modestly rejected this offer, but indicated that he would accept the position of commander in chief of the Nicaraguan army.

During his first few days in Granada, for the sake of convenience Walker stayed at the house of a captivating though overripe femme fatale known as "Niña Irena." This gracious

WALKER'S TROOPS RESTING AFTER THE BATTLE IN GRANADA

lady of Spanish-Irish descent had been a favorite of numerous
Legitimist officers for years. Apart from her fading beauty, she
possessed a keen, penetrating intellect and a wily fondness for
intrigue. She concentrated all her charms on the hero of the
moment, William Walker, but to no avail. The cold little filibuster refused to yield to her tender advances. He wanted no
part of her and suspected in fact that she still had Legitimist
sympathies. So he soon moved out of Niña Irena's house to
austere bachelor's quarters in the Government House on the
plaza.

Walker now turned his attention to peace negotiations with
General Ponciano Corral, who commanded the Legitimist
troops at Rivas, a force of some one thousand men. John H.
Wheeler, the United States minister to Nicaragua, agreed to
visit Corral and try to work out a peace treaty, but was rebuffed
and insulted in this diplomatic effort.

GENERAL WALKER REVIEWING HIS TROOPS IN THE GRAND PLAZA,
GRANADA, CAPITAL OF NICARAGUA

An incident later forced Corral to come to terms, however. A transit steamer from San Francisco arrived at San Juan del Sur carrying some sixty American filibusters under the command of Parker H. French. French marched his volunteers over the Transit Road to Virgin Bay and placed them aboard a lake steamer, where they mingled with the civilian passengers,

A SQUAD OF WALKER'S MEN AT VIRGIN BAY

including women and children. He then ordered the ship to attempt to capture Fort San Carlos, on the other side of the lake. When he found that this fort was too strongly defended by the Legitimists, however, French went back across the lake to Granada and reported with his volunteers to Walker. The steamer returned to Virgin Bay with about 250 passengers, who were sheltered in the Accessory Transit Company's buildings. Some Legitimist soldiers, finding it difficult to distinguish between gringo filibusters and gringo passengers, fired on this group, killing and wounding several innocent travelers. To make matters worse, other Legitimist soldiers at Fort San Carlos, having been alerted, opened fire on the next transit steamer coming up the San Juan River from the Caribbean and inadvertently killed a woman and a child.

Walker decided that these barbarous acts by the Legitimists called for retaliation and stern punishment, to set an example and prevent any such recurrences. The Filibuster ordered a prominent Legitimist cabinet member, Don Mateo Mayorga, to be executed by a firing squad in the main plaza of Granada. The families of many prominent Legitimist officers were still residing in Granada, and Walker threatened to kill more hostages. General Corral therefore decided he had to come to Walker and try to make peace in order to avoid further reprisals.

Walker proposed a peace treaty, but Corral wrote most of it. This treaty, signed October 23, 1855, suspended the Nicaraguan war between the Legitimists—symbolized by the white ribbon—and the Democrats—the red ribbon; a compromise blue emblem was substituted, bearing the words NICARAGUA INDEPENDIENTE. Patricio Rivas, a moderate Legitimist, was named provisional president of Nicaragua; Corral became minister of war; the new commander in chief of the Nicaraguan army was General William Walker.

A few days later the solemn inauguration of the new government took place in the main church of Granada. The dark building was illuminated by devotional candles as the highest-ranking officials, including President Rivas and General Walker, knelt in fitting humility before a crucifix and were sworn in. Padre Agustín Vijil, a prominent local priest who later enthusiastically supported Walker, conducted the religious ceremony. (Legitimists who were not directly threatened by Walker denounced the new coalition and condemned Vijil as a collaborator.)

Within four months after landing in Nicaragua with fifty-eight soldiers of fortune, William Walker had taken over as virtual dictator of the nation. Nicaragua was at peace, if only temporarily and uncomfortably.

Having acquired some old type and a printing press in Granada, Walker decided to publish a weekly propaganda newspaper, *El Nicaraguense,* to publicize the peaceful beauty and brilliant future of Nicaragua. The text was partly in Spanish but mostly in English. Walker was described as the "regenerator" and "gray-eyed man of destiny," who had arrived in Nicaragua as a friend of the poor and oppressed and had been welcomed by the local population with joyful enthusiasm.

Many years before Walker's arrival in Central America several European travelers had recorded that there was an old traditional belief among the Mosquito Indians in eastern Nicaragua: that they would be delivered or saved from the dark-complexioned Spanish oppressors by a gray-eyed man. This mysterious prophecy by a heathen oracle may have made a deep impression on Walker. In any event, it was the source of the popular description of the Filibuster as the "gray-eyed man of destiny."

The tranquil idyll of peace at Granada lasted but a few days. Walker's iron discipline was soon to be tested again: one of his own filibusters, an Irish-American from the slums of New York named Patrick Jordan, intoxicated by too much aguardiente, went on a shooting spree on the streets of Granada that resulted in the death of an innocent native. Walker immediately ordered a court-martial to make an example of this unruly culprit, since stern justice had to be applied to all. Just before he was shot at sunrise, on November 1, 1855, Jordan delivered a moving address to his companions in arms in which he warned them against the evils of hard liquor and acknowledged the justice of his own death sentence—which he hoped would serve as an example to others.

A week later more blood flowed. The temporary uneasy truce between the Legitimists and Democrats was broken by

DURING SEVERAL CENTURIES BEFORE THE ARRIVAL OF WILLIAM
WALKER IN 1855, A LEGEND HAD EXISTED AMONG THE MOSQUITO
INDIANS OF NICARAGUA THAT A "GRAY-EYED STRANGER" WOULD
COME TO THEIR SHORES AND BECOME THEIR LEADER

General Corral, who felt his authority in the army was slipping—
even the Legitimist power was now in the hands of Walker and
the hated Democratic opposition of León.

The time had come to plead urgently for stronger military
assistance from the neighboring republics in order to oust the
gringo filibusters. Corral wrote three secret letters requesting,
in no uncertain terms, the immediate armed intervention of
Guatemala and Honduras and emphasizing the serious danger
of Walker's presence in Central America. Corral's three
letters, entrusted to a messenger with grievances against the
Legitimists, soon fell into Walker's hands. To make matters
worse for Corral, one of the fatal letters was addressed to
General Santos Guardiola in Honduras.

The commander in chief called a cabinet meeting which Corral, not suspecting danger, made the mistake of attending. Walker laid the incriminating letters before President Rivas and the rest of the cabinet. Corral turned pale, but admitted with dignity that he had indeed written the letters. Walker requested President Rivas to arrest Corral, charging him with treason and conspiracy to overturn the government of the republic. Unwilling to trust his fate to the judgment of his fellow countrymen, Corral, at his own request, was tried by a body of American officers presided over by Colonel C. C. Hornsby. He was found guilty and sentenced to death.

The citizens of Granada were stunned: Corral was a popular local hero. The sympathy of the people for the condemned prisoner, including the fervent pleas and sobs of Corral's daughters, had little effect upon Walker, who forthwith approved the death sentence. The idol of the Nicaraguan Legitimists was shot in the grand plaza of Granada, standing, facing a firing squad made up of American *falanginos*. Dozens of Corral's admirers rushed to the quivering corpse of the patriotic martyr to dip their handkerchiefs in his blood and clip locks of his hair as memorabilia.

Walker had disposed of a formidable political enemy and had suddenly become the strongest leader in Nicaragua. He had gained the support of the Nicaraguan Liberals and Southern admirers in the United States, who looked greedily at Central American territories that might be annexed to extend slavery. Some Northerners in the United States also still approved of Walker as a champion of Manifest Destiny. But the Filibuster had alienated the Nicaraguan Legitimists, the other Central American republics, who feared him, and Great Britain, which resented his intrusion on the isthmus.

Forty-eight hours after the execution of Corral the new Nicaraguan government created by Walker was prematurely recognized by the American minister, John Wheeler, a friend and admirer of Walker's. The normal delay in communications had caused Wheeler's official instructions to arrive too late; when they came, Washington, adhering to the Clayton-Bulwer

IN NOVEMBER 1855 WILLIAM WALKER EXECUTED THE
LEGITIMIST LEADER, GENERAL PONCIANO CORRAL, FOR TREASON
Walker thus became the undisputed head of the Nicaraguan government five months after landing in that country with fifty-eight soldiers
of fortune.

Treaty, belatedly ordered Wheeler not to recognize the new
government. United States recognition was subsequently
withdrawn and Wheeler reprimanded.

The State Department was constantly being embarrassed
by William Walker. It was obvious that there was a great deal
of pro-Walker sympathy in the United States, but the government in Washington wanted to avoid a direct confrontation
with Britain. On December 8, 1855, Franklin Pierce issued a
proclamation against filibustering in which he warned all citizens who were considering departing from the United States
to participate in military operations in the state of Nicaragua,

either singly or in groups, contrary to their duty as good citizens and thus threatening the peace of the United States, that they would do so at their own risk: they would cease to be protected by the United States government. Furthermore, he called on all officers, having lawful powers civil and military, to prevent such disreputable and criminal undertakings.

In December 1855 Walker sent a so-called minister to Washington to plead his cause. This representative, Parker H. French, although he was a charming conversationalist, turned out to be an unfortunate choice. First, Secretary of State William Marcy refused to see him. Then it came to light that French was a glib swindler and charlatan, known as "one-armed French"

PARKER H. FRENCH

Although William Walker himself was scrupulously honest and not interested in financial gain, some of his followers had different goals. Parker H. French was appointed Nicaraguan minister to the United States by Walker in late 1855. French had been guilty of forgery and embezzlement in Texas several years earlier. The American government's refusal to recognize him embarrassed Walker.

Department of State,
Washington, December 21, 1855.

Parker H. French, Esquire,
Washington.

Sir:

Your letter to me of the 19th. instant with the enclosed copy of "an autograph letter from the President of Nicaragua to the President of the United States of America" has been received, and laid before the President. I am directed by him to reply to your communication that he has not yet seen reasons for establishing diplomatic intercourse with the persons who now claim to exercise the political power in the State of Nicaragua.

Those who were chiefly instrumental in suspending or overthrowing the former government of that State were not citizens belonging to it, nor have those citizens, or any considerable part of them, so far as is known here, freely expressed their approval of or acquiesced in the present condition of the political affairs of Nicaragua. Until such shall appear to be the case, the President does not deem it proper to receive you or any one as a Minister to this government duly appointed by the Supreme Government of Nicaragua.

I am, Sir, Your obedient servant.
W. S. Marcy.

SECRETARY OF STATE MARCY'S LETTER TO PARKER H. FRENCH REFUSING RECOGNITION OF WALKER'S GOVERNMENT IN NICARAGUA (he had lost his right arm in a gunfight in Mexico). In 1850 he had forged a two-thousand-dollar letter of credit in San Antonio, Texas, in order to purchase government supplies. After this ugly report had been resurrected, French returned to Nicaragua under a cloud. Walker received him coldly, then dismissed him.

The other Central American republics were astounded when Secretary of State Marcy rejected French and refused to recognize the new government of Nicaragua on the grounds that the persons instrumental in overthrowing the old regime in Nicaragua were not citizens of that country. It was hard for the governments of Guatemala, Costa Rica, Honduras, and El Salvador to believe that William Walker did not have the official backing of the United States government: after all, only seven years had elapsed since the war between the United States and Mexico. This judgment by Secretary of State Marcy unquestionably encouraged and strengthened the hands of the anti-Walker forces in Central America.

Walker's political ambition was not limited to Central America. Had he been able to consolidate his victories in Nicaragua, he planned to attack Cuba in cooperation with a group of Cuban exiles represented by Captain F. A. Lainé, according to the following excerpts of a contract signed by Walker and Lainé in January 1856:

> General William Walker, Commander-in-Chief of the army of Nicaragua is willing to form the following agreement with Captain F. A. Lainé, appointed agent of Sr. Domingo de Goicouria, sole holder and depository of the goods and chattels belonging to the cause of Cuba, consisting in money, a vessel and munitions of war.
>
> *Firstly*—General William Walker pledges his word of honor that he will assist and cooperate with his person and with his various resources, such as men and others, in the cause of Cuba, and in favor of liberty, after having consolidated the peace and Government of the Republic of Nicaragua.
>
> *Secondly*—General William Walker proposed and admits the understanding that the material and pecuniary resources of Nicaragua as well as those which are in the possession of the revolutionary party of Cuba, shall be amalgamated together, making common cause together for the purpose of overthrowing the Spanish tyranny in the island, and of insuring the prosperity of Central America.

Domingo de Goicouria, a Cuban revolutionary leader known as "the Liberator," was for a time a brigadier general in Walker's army. He enlisted 250 recruits for service in Walker's cause and managed to persuade Cornelius Vanderbilt to advance the cost of their passage to Nicaragua. It was tacitly understood that Walker later was supposed to help the Cubans win the independence of their island from Spain. As it turned out, Walker was never in a position to launch an invasion of Cuba: he was far too preoccupied with troubles in Central America.

The Filibuster appealed to the other four Central American republics for peaceful coexistence and urged them to lay down their arms. This request fell on deaf ears, since it was well known that Walker was attempting to increase the size of his own army by recruiting more North American volunteers. Recruiting offices were opened up in San Francisco. Additional North Americans, mostly from the Pacific and Southern states, enlisted in his cause. Many volunteers purchased through tickets from San Francisco to New York, and stopped off at Nicaragua to indulge in a little filibustering. The Accessory Transit Company cooperated with Walker: hundreds of "emigrants" were transported to Nicaragua from both New York and San Francisco at the bargain price of twenty dollars a head; some even traveled free.

Ne'er-do-well idlers and adventurers, attracted by visions of easy booty, were destined to be disillusioned by Walker's strict, Prussian-like discipline. Debauchery and even profanity were vices not to be tolerated and brought severe punishment to unruly perpetrators. The well-behaved were rewarded by their monthly pay of twenty-five dollars—if and when it was available, for Walker's treasury was often drained—plus a title to up to 350 acres of land, contingent on success in subduing the country.

The following firsthand report from *Harper's Weekly* of March 14, 1857, illustrates the disillusionment of many recruits after their arrival in Nicaragua:

Let us turn now to another aspect of filibusterism—the light in which it appears to the mere military adventurer; the man out of employ-

EL NICARAGUENSE.

VOL. 1. GRANADA, SATURDAY, MAY 31, 1856. NO. 30.

El Nicaraguense.

PUBLISHED SATURDAY MORNINGS.

PRICE TWO DIMES.

JOHN TABOR, Proprietor.

REGULAR TERMS :

For one copy, per annum,.......... $8 00
For one copy six months,.......... 4 50
For one copy three months,........ 2 40

☞ Advertisements inserted at the rate of two
dollars and fifty cents per square of eight lines for
the first, and a reduction of one dollar for each
subsequent insertion.

☞ Liberal arrangements made with monthly
and yearly advertisers.

☞ Job Printing of every description executed with neatness and despatch, and on reasonable
terms.

Office in Front of the Plaza.

BY WINES & CO.'S EXPRESS.

NEWS FROM THE EAST.

NICARAGUA STOCK AT PAR!

Men and Money for Gen. Walker.

Reception of Padre Vijil.

RECOGNITION OF OUR INDEPENDENCE.

Enthusiasm in the U. States!

Monster Meetings in N. York and N. Orleans.

Between October 1855 and November 1856 a curious pro-American weekly newspaper was published in Granada, Nicaragua, by William Walker. Known as "El Nicaraguense" and printed partly in Spanish but mostly in English, this remarkable publication, composed hastily under difficult conditions, outlined the Filibuster's plans to regenerate Nicaragua.

Its propaganda stressed Walker's political and military victories, while overlooking his troubles and defeats.

Copies were sent regularly to the United States in an attempt to lure recruits to Walker's service in beautiful, exotic Nicaragua.

Some interesting excerpts from "El Nicaraguense" are reproduced herewith, including a colonization decree granting 250 acres to colonists, dated November 23, 1855; an announcement of William Walker's election and inauguration as president of Nicaragua in July 1856; a public advertisement, dated August 23, 1856, of a commissioner's sale at which expropriated properties of Walker's political enemies were to be sold at public auction; a report from Chile, dated October 18, 1856, according to which the Spanish-American states were going to join together to resist the white race of North America and especially General Walker in Nicaragua; a warning to deserters from Walker's army in Nicaragua; and some typical newspaper advertisements of the day for the local citizens of Granada.

The last issue of "El Nicaraguense" was published on November 22, 1856. The disastrous siege and burning of Granada brought about the demise of the newspaper when the printing press was destroyed.

El Nicaraguense

PUBLISHED SATURDAY MORNINGS.

PRICE TWO DIMES.

JOHN TABOR, Proprietor.

REGULAR TERMS :

For one copy, per annum,.......... $8 00
For one copy six months,.......... 4 50
For one copy three months,........ 2 40

☞ Advertisements inserted at the rate of two
dollars and fifty cents per square of eight lines for
the first, and a reduction of one dollar for each
subsequent insertion.

☞ Liberal arrangements made with monthly
and yearly advertisers.

☞ Job Printing of every description executed with neatness and despatch, and on reasonable
terms.

Office in Front of the Plaza.

FOUNDERS OF THE REPUBLIC.

PAY-ROLL

Of the Original Fifty-Eight, under Gen. Walker, from May 4th, 1855, to July 1st, 1856,
Showing their names, Date of Enlistment, Term of Service, Wages per month, Quarter-Master's Account, Pay due, with a few Remarks as to their Promotions, Deaths, and Discharges.

Names.	Date of Enlistment.	No. of months.	No. of days.	Rate per month.	Total amount.	Q'rmaster' Account.	Balance.	Remarks.
Gen. Wm. Walker,	May 4, 1855.	7	10	100 00	$733 33			Amount due to Dec. 14, 1855.
Gen. Wm. Walker, Commander in Chief,		6	10	500 00	3266 66			" from Dec. 14, 1855, to July 1, 1856.
					4000 00	$4000 00		
Col. C. C. Hornsby,	May 4, 1855	7	10	100 00	733 33			Amount due to Dec. 14, 1855.
Col. C. C. Hornsby,			28	65 00	186 66			Colonel's pay from above date to Jan. 12, 1856;
Brig. Gen. C. C. Hornsby,		5	18	300 00	1680 00			Brig. Generals pay from last date to July 1, 1856.
					2600 00	2600 00		
Col. A Jones, Surgeon-General,	May 4, 1855.		10	100 00	733 33			Amount due to Dec. 14, 1855.
Col. A. Jones, Paymaster General,		6	10	200 00	1306 66			Colonel's pay from above date to July 1, 1856.
					2040 0	2040 00		

Arrival of the Steamer.

The La Virgin arrived at the wharf last evening, bringing the mails by the Daniel Webster from New Orleans, with dates up to the 23d of July.

The news is of the stalest character imaginable. Politics has absorbed all attention in the States.

Mr. Phillip R. Toohey, one of the unfortunate prisoners wounded and taken at Santa Rosa, has arrived in New Orleans, and is lecturing and writing in favor of this Republic.

El Nicaraguense.

Saturday Morning, Nov. 15.

ANOTHER TRIUMPH OF AMERICANS !

Total Route of the Enemy, with great Loss of Life !

PARTICULARS OF THE FIRST ATTACK UNDER BRIG. GEN. HORNSBY.

GALLANT CHARGE OF THE 1st AND 2d RIFLES.

Bravery of the Infantry.

Advance of Gen. Walker in Person !

El Nicaraguense.

Saturday Morning, August 23.

HACIENDAS FOR SALE.

COMMISSIONERS' SALE.

PURSUANT to an order issued by the Board of Commissioners, I will, on the FIRST DAY OF JANUARY, 1857, offer the following inventoried property for sale at public auction, on the Plaza in the city of Granada.

Terms—Cash or Military Script.

The sale will continue from day to day until the whole is disposed of.

Parties desirous of seeing the property and examining for themselves will be furnished with notices and guides by application at my office.

Class of Property.	Name of Estates.	Property of	Remarks.	Value.
Hacienda de Cacao,	Rosario,	José Antonio Lopez,	Trees in full bearing,	$14,000
Do. do.	Candelaria,	Do.	Young trees,	10,000
Do. Cattle,	Las Cruz,	Do.	A row of six stores,	1,500
house in Rivas,		Do.		10,000
hacienda de Cacao				
and Indigo,	Pital,	Juan José Ruiz,		8,000
hacienda de Cacao,	Paraiso,	Do.		14,000
Do. Indigo,	Jesus Maria,	Do.		1,800
house in Rivas,		Do.	Large adobe,	8,000
hacienda de Cacao,	San Francisco,	José J. Arguello Arce		18,000
Do. do.		Do.	Abandoned estate,	600
house in Granada,		Do.		8,000
hacienda de Cacao,		Yudilacio Maleaño,		21,000
house in Granada,				10,000
hacienda de Cacao,	Pital,	Francisco Guerra,		18,000
house and lot in Rivas,		Do.		2,000
houses in Rivas,		Do.	Row partially burnt.	10,000
hacienda de Cacao,	Santa Fé,	José M. Maleaño,		18,000
cattle Estate,	Juan Davila,	Do.		5,000
house in Rivas,		Do.	Long row,	7,000
hacienda de Cacao,		Felipe & S. Saenz,	Near Tolo—some wild lands,	3,000
Do. do.	El Viejo,	Clemente Santos,	Old estate, near Rivas,	1,000
houses in Rivas,		Do.	Large adobe,	10,000
houses and property in				
San Juan del Sur,		Felipe Aviles,		8,000
hacienda de Cacao,		Do.	With wild lands,	8,000
Do. do.	Salitre,	Do.		
Haciendas de Cacao,	Jocote—LaGalpa,	F. & E. Carazo.		27,000
hacienda de Cacao,	David,	D. Lopez & B. Darce,		7,000
Do. do.		B. & José Caracus,	Two-thirds of the estate,	2,800
Do. do.	Esperanza,	P. Rivas & family,		8,000
Do. Do.	Chitala,	José Alfaro,	Contain ng 150 acres,	2,000
houses in Rivas		Do.		1,800

Parte Española.

Sábado, Agosto 9 de 1856.

SE PUBLICARA

TODOS LOS SABADOS,

TERMINOS DE SUSCRIPCION:

Por una copia, el año, ... $ 8 00
Por una copia suelta, ... 20

TERMINOS ADVIRTIENDO:

Por una cuartillo de ocho lineas, primera
nsercion, ... $2 50
Cada insercion consecuente, ... 1 50

A LA JUVENTUD.

Dignos por mas de un título de ocupar un lugar en las columas del *Nicaraguense*, reproducimos á continuacion los párrafos de un artículo publicado

---

DECREE.

THE Supreme Government of the Republic of Nicaragua to encourage the immigration of persons of thrift and industry to become settlers and inhabitants within its territorial limits, to the end that its resources may be fully developed and its commerce increased, and to promote the general welfare of the State, has decreed:

Art. 1. A free donation or grant of 250 acres of public land shall be made to each single person who shall enter the State (during the continuance of this decree) and settle and make improvements upon the said tract, the same to be located by the Director of Colonization hereafter to be named, and immediate possession given.

Art. 2. Each family entering the State and settling upon its territory shall receive 100 acres of land in addition to the 250 granted to single settlers.

Art. 3. A right to occupy and improve shall be issued to applicants, and at the expiration of six months, upon satisfactory evidence being presented to the Director of Colonization of compliance with the provisions of this decree, title will be given.

Art. 4. No duties shall be levied on the personal effects, household furniture, agricultural implements, seeds, plants, domestic animals, or other imports for the personal use of the colonists or the development of the resources of the land donated, and colonists shall be exempt from all extraordinary taxes, and contributions, and from all public service except when the public safety shall otherwise demand.

Art. 5. The colonists being citizens of the Republic cannot alienate the land granted to any foreign government whatever, and shall not alienate the said land or their rights thereunto until after an occupancy of at least six months.

Art. 6. A colonization office shall be established and a Director of Colonization appointed, whose business it shall be to attend to the application from the emigrants, to collect and dispense seeds, plants, &c., and to keep the Registry Books of the Department.

Done in Granada, the 23d of November 1855.
PATRICIO RIVAS,
President of the Republic.

REPUBLIC OF NICARAGUA,
DEPARTMENT OF STATE,
GRANADA, July 11, 1856.

Sir—The Supreme Executive Power has been pleased to dictate the following decree:—

Fermin Ferrer, Provisional President of the Republic of Nicaragua, to its inhabitants:—

The Presidential elections, which are to rule the destinies of the nation, having been effected in conformity with the decree bearing date of the 10th ultimo, and having in view the returns of the different electoral districts, forwarded by the cities of the Republic, and having executed the accustomed scrutiny of the candidates which appear in said returns, I have been pleased to decree and do

DECREE.

1. Declared elected by a majority of votes as President of the Republic of Nicaragua, General William Walker.

2. That the same be announced in the most solemn manner, and communicated to the elected candidate, who shall take possession of his office on the 12th day of the present month.

Given in Granada, this 10th day of July, 1856.
F. FERRER.

GRANADA. SATURDAY, JULY 19, 1856.

INAUGURATION OF WILLIAM WALKER AS PRESIDENT.

INAUGURACION

DEL

PRESIDENTE WILLIAM WALKER.

El Nicaraguense.

Saturday Morning, Oct. 18.

COMBINATION OF ALL THE SPANISH AMERICAN STATES AGAINST THE WHITE RACE.

A Chilian newspaper, "El Diario," published at Valparaiso, which claims to be the "Organ of National Progress," in a long article published in its columns on Sept. 1, 1856, takes strong ground in favor of a combination of all the Hispanio-American States to resist what it calls the filibustering tendencies of the government at Washington, and the whole white race of North America.

But, before all things, says El Diario, comfort is necessary for those who are suffering in Nicaragua under the power of Gen. Walker. On the floor of the Chilian House of Representatives, ten members have protested against the leaning of the Cabinet at Washington, for the purpose of exciting an interest in the Hispanio-American countries, and in the hope of being the means of forming a protecting alliance by the unity of their race.

El Nicaraguense.

Saturday Morning, Nov. 22.

ADVANCE ON MASAYA!

Attempted Ambuscade of the Enemy!

THEIR TOTAL ROUTE!

ENTRANCE TO MASAYA.

STORMING OF THE CHURCH!

Repulse of Opposing Forces.

THE BURNING OF THE TOWN.

Possession of Part of the Large Plaza.

GREAT DANGER OF SICKNESS.

Withdrawal of the Troops.

A WARNING TO DESERTERS.

After the Allied forces had been routed at the battles fought on the Transit, some of our men, while roaming about in the woods adjacent to the scene of conflict, found the body of a white man, whom they at once recognized as having at one time belonged to the Nicaraguan Army, but had deserted to the ranks of the enemy. It would appear they had used the unfortunate man as a guide, and after he had piloted them to the spot, showed them the strong points, and served them until he was no longer of any use to them, they tied his legs together by a strong rope, and then having shot the whole of the top of his head off, left his body to be picked up and buried by his countrymen and former associates.

Whatever may be the expectations of those who leave the ranks of the Nicaraguan Army for those of the Allies, or whatever inducements may be held out to them in order to persuade them to take this step, they will surely meet their fate when their services are no longer required.

ment, who allows himself to be recruited for the want of something better to do. He passes under the name of a colonist, and it may be some vague idea of cultivating or selling a quarter section of land in Central America has presented itself to his mind. He is informed by some agent of General Walker that his passage will be given free to him if he will confer the favor of his presence, and consent to shoulder a musket. He really imagines that in going he is conferring a favor; but when he arrives in the land of promise, a very different view is taken of the matter by his employers. During the passage up the river from San Juan to Virgin Bay he had heard evil rumors in regard to the situation of the filibuster army; enough to satisfy him that the country and the service he has gone into are not to be considered a paradise. He resolves to go back, but finds that it is quite impossible to do so. By accepting the free passage he has bound himself, body and soul, to the fortunes of the adventurer. His name on the immigration list, placed there by himself or by others, is the signature by which he is bound for evil or good. He discovers, too late, that it is not for "one hundred and sixty acres," nor for "$25 a month;" but simply for nothing a month, and six feet of earth.

THE SOLDIER

Arriving at Virgin Bay, he and his confederates are marched into quarters, or directed to report themselves to somebody who bears a commission from "his Excellency." Perhaps the immigrant has *not* accepted a free passage, but through magnanimity or through prudence has paid his fare. Announcing, however, his willingness to serve as a soldier, provided the service is agreeable, he allows his name to go upon a list of volunteers, or by some contrivance it has been placed there without his knowledge. Refusing to march in consequence, he is treated with severity, and he applies to "his Excellency" in person; but his representations are met with contempt. In an agony of rage and apprehension he rushes to the office of the American Consul or Minister, and demands redress, as a citizen of the United States. The Consul, or the Minister, very quietly informs him that "there is no remedy;" that the rights of American citizens in Nicaragua are entirely ignored; and that "his Excellency" has positively requested that no passports be issued. He applies to the agents of the Transit Company; they will tell him that "it is impossible to buy tickets for New York or San Francisco without a passport." After beating his wings for a while against his prison bars, our involuntary filibuster marches off sullenly to his barracks, and resigns himself to a short allowance of boiled beef and plantains.

THE BARRACK

Here he finds a number of unhappy wretches, like himself, subject to the profane tyranny of a drunken sergeant. He is now a man without the recognition or the privilege of a man; the tenant of a dirty kennel, with earth or boards for a bed, fleas and vermin for his intimate friends, and fulsome oaths and unparalleled obscenity for his daily conversation; his diet, a perpetual ration of bad beef, cooked by himself and others equally unfit, in foul vessels, with the rare accident of a hard biscuit. He is now a hewer of wood and a drawer of water. His habitation, dignified by the name of a barrack or "quarters"—a shed of boards or of mud—has been half torn away by its previous occupants to furnish coffins for the dead, or fuel for the camp-kettle. It is surrounded by a wide area of excrementitious offenses, the tokens of laziness and disease. After ten or fourteen days of hardships and disgusts, extreme and intolerable when compared with the meanest life of civilization, his low spirits, bad food, and constant exposure to dirt, heat, and the annoyance of an earth or plank floor, will have ripened his blood for the all-pervading and unavoidable fever. He sleeps in his daily clothing. At night, the wind of the lake chills him; and by day, the tropical heat withers. A diarrhea, a dysentery, or a calentura commences. After a time—it may be the third or fourth week—he fades into the hospital. "Leave all hope, ye that enter here!" for, as hell is to purgatory, so is the hospital to the barrack.

When the company is turned out for daily drill, with the rifle or the musket, it presents a motley file, such as Falstaff swore he would not march with "through Coventry." Thieves, cut-throats, and honest men, like an Algerine galley-gang of white slaves—with the notable difference that the honest man has been gulled into this deadly trap, by his own countrymen, with promises of pay, land, and glory.

So has it been at Virgin Bay, Granada, and elsewhere in Nicaragua; and the most fortunate have been those who fell, in battle by a sudden death; the many thousands of the sick and the wounded dying miserably of suffering and privation.

A New York newspaper columnist suggested that it would be a fine thing if Walker's recruiting in that city were an outstanding success: it would be an ideal way to get rid of bums, loafers, criminals, and other worthless ruffians. Texas had formerly been the place for these restless vagabonds, and "G.T.T.—gone to Texas!" was the cry; then they were drawn to California, until the San Francisco Vigilance Committee was organized; now it was filibustering with Walker in Nicaragua. Besides being a blessing for New York, it even gave the volunteers the satisfaction of dying in a good cause, something they would never have the shadow of a chance of doing at home. Send them down to Walker!

William Walker was not the only North American filibuster interested in Nicaragua in 1855: Colonel Henry L. Kinney from

Pennsylvania and Texas had his own "colonization" enterprise in Mosquitia, or the Mosquito Coast, based upon a grant bestowed upon him by the Mosquito king. Its history was not promising. A dismal, swampy, unhealthy and sparsely populated area in eastern Nicaragua, Mosquitia had attracted few missionaries. Its uncharted shoreline, however, offered favorable hiding places for seventeenth- and eighteenth-century pirates, mostly English. The natives, known as Mosquito Indians, were a mixture of Negro and Indian. The population was gradually increased by fugitive slaves from the West Indies, augmented by a large cargo of Africans who found refuge there following the wreck of a slave ship.

In 1687 the governor of Jamaica decided to make the Mosquito Coast into a protectorate, so a native Mosquito chief was taken to Jamaica, dressed up in the latest European fashion, and named the king of the Mosquitoes. Accepting—somewhat reluctantly—a paper commission and a cocked hat, the new king placed his kingdom under the protection of Great Britain.

By 1839 a later Mosquito king, Robert Charles Frederick, had shown his skill as a royal trader by giving away various sections of his kingdom in return for barrels of rum, whisky, and other costly merchandise. One of these grants included a large portion of eastern Nicaragua and Costa Rica, including much of the San Juan River. The recipients of this grant, two British subjects named Samuel and Peter Shepherd, then sold it in 1850 to Colonel Kinney, a veteran of the Mexican War. The Kinney enterprise is reported to have purchased 22 million acres in exchange for a promissory note in the amount of $500,000. Kinney attempted unsuccessfully to sell stock in his company in order to raise money for a grandiose colonization and farming development on the Mosquito Coast, where he offered fertile tropical land at the bargain price of twenty-five cents per acre.

Following considerable publicity, some five hundred emigrants were supposed to sail from New York with Kinney on May 7, 1855, on the fast new steamer *United States*. Kinney had been a real estate entrepreneur in Texas, where he was one of the wealthy "proprietors and owners" of the thriving town of Corpus Christi, according to *Leslie's*. On the East Coast, however, he was no match for the owners of the Accessory Transit Company, who decided to thwart him and block his project—the transit company did not want any competition around Greytown that might interfere with the transit monopoly. The transit company officials apparently had powerful friends in Washington: Kinney was indicted by a federal grand jury, arrested, and charged with organizing a military expedition against Nicaragua.

When Kinney was released on bail, the *United States* was blockaded by federal vessels to prevent its departure. His followers became demoralized, and when Kinney finally left New York, on the small schooner *Emma* (sailing surreptitiously to avoid arrest), he had only thirteen companions. En route to Greytown the *Emma* ran aground and was wrecked. When Kinney finally reached that gloomy, miserable village of fifty squalid huts, he was a sick, ruined financier. Although he managed to get himself elected civil and military governor of Greytown, it was to no avail: several fellow colonizers soon deserted him in order to join William Walker at Granada, late in 1855.

Kinney himself then attempted to join the Filibuster, but was bitterly disappointed. Walker regarded Kinney as an imposter and potential enemy of his own Nicaraguan government, who might interfere with Atlantic communications by blocking the entrance to the San Juan River. The indignant Filibuster reportedly exclaimed: "Tell Colonel Kinney, or Governor Kinney, or Mr. Kinney, or whatever he is called, that if I ever catch him in Nicaragua I'll hang him."

Despite this warning Kinney decided to visit Granada anyway, since his own situation was so desperate. On February 8, 1856, President Rivas, at Walker's instigation, issued a decree that the Mosquito Coast belonged to Nicaragua and that Kinney's claims to any part of it were null and void.

Three days later Walker granted Kinney an audience, arranged by two of the Filibuster's officers who had known Kinney

COL. HENRY L. KINNEY

In 1850 Kinney was reputed to be one of the proprietors and owners of the thriving town of Corpus Christi, Texas. He tried unsuccessfully to colonize the Mosquito Coast of eastern Nicaragua. William Walker opposed him.

previously. The preliminary discussions were quite polite, but the situation changed overnight when Walker learned that Kinney, in a secret rendezvous, had warned President Rivas that Walker's army would devour Nicaragua like a plague of locusts, and that it would be far better for Rivas to favor Kinney's own colonists.

The following morning Kinney, a large, corpulent man, presented himself, smiling and optimistic. His mood soon changed as the frowning Filibuster, in his typically quiet, reserved style stated: "Mr. Kinney, you have used improper methods in discussing government affairs. I have ordered your arrest."

Kinney, turning red in the face, shouted: "You can't arrest me. I came here on a guarantee of safe conduct."

Sure enough, Walker ascertained that such a pledge had indeed been given by Carlos Thomas, his treasurer-general. Walker, instead of hanging Kinney, ordered that he be taken back to Greytown under an armed guard.

Kinney's attempted colonization project on the Mosquito Coast failed ignominiously. Broken in health and impoverished, he returned to the United States. But bad luck continued to pursue Kinney: in 1861 he was killed in a gunfight in Matamoros, Mexico.

A CENTRAL AMERICAN LIEUTENANT ON MULEBACK

10

A Serious Error

IN EARLY 1856 William Walker committed the most serious error of his erratic career. He picked a quarrel with the mighty Commodore Cornelius Vanderbilt, the second-richest man in the United States (William B. Astor, son of John Jacob Astor, was the richest). Conceivably if Walker had managed to keep Vanderbilt as an ally and had cooperated with him, Nicaragua might eventually have become Americanized. But the virtually penniless Walker, following unsound legal advice given by his friend Edmund Randolph, grossly underestimated Vanderbilt's power and incredible wealth. It was for this apparent indifference to the realities of American life that Horace Greeley, founder of the *New York Tribune*, called William Walker the "Don Quixote of Central America." Walker seemed to be tilting in vain at the omnipotent windmill of money power, which he did not comprehend.

Two unscrupulous commercial rivals of Vanderbilt's—Charles Morgan and C. K. Garrison—wished to gain control of the transit route themselves. They persuaded Walker to seize the boats and other property of the Accessory Transit Company in the name of the Nicaraguan government, to cover a large debt the transit company allegedly owed Nicaragua. Domingo de Goicouria tried in vain to prevail upon Walker to enlist Vanderbilt's powerful financial support, instead of taking a stand against such a formidable opponent. Why kill the goose that lays the golden eggs? But the filibuster leader was naive

118

in financial matters, and besides, he may have felt that Vanderbilt had slighted him. So Walker foolishly sided with the underdogs Morgan and Garrison. Brigadier General Goicouria was punished for his interference by being dropped from the roster of the Nicaraguan army.

Following Walker's instructions, President Rivas of Nicaragua willingly signed the decree revoking the charter of the Accessory Transit Company on February 18, 1856. This news was held up, however, so that Morgan in New York could secretly be informed of this act one steamer ahead of the general public.

Walker wanted Morgan and Garrison to receive this communication before Vanderbilt did, so that the two conspirators could arrange as soon as possible to put new steamers on the Nicaragua route to bring down additional recruits and supplies. Morgan, however, was primarily interested in the confidential message in order to make a killing on Wall Street at the expense of his archrival Vanderbilt. Acting for Garrison and himself, Morgan not only sold out their entire holdings in the Accessory Transit Company but went short the stock; Vanderbilt and his group, meanwhile, were just as actively buying the shares, little realizing that the filibuster movement was acting against their interests. On March 12, the day before the steamer arrived from Nicaragua with the report that the charter had been annulled and a new one granted to Edmund Randolph (that is, Morgan and Garrison), the stock of the Accessory Transit Company sold at twenty-two dollars per share. A few days later, after the news arrived in New York, this same stock sold off to about thirteen dollars, and Morgan covered his short position at a huge profit. Vanderbilt and his associates, having lost heavily, were infuriated and soon thirsting for revenge.

This was the turning point in Walker's life, although of course he did not realize it at the time. The *New York Herald* succinctly warned that it was in Mr. Vanderbilt's power to kill off the new Nicaraguan government by opening another route and thus cutting off Walker's communications with San Francisco and New York. This is precisely what happened.

OFFICE OF NICARAGUA
STEAMSHIP COMPANY
IN SAN FRANCISCO, 1854

NICARAGUA
STEAMSHIP COMPAN

— FOR —

NEW YORK AND NEW ORLEA
DIRECT,

VIA SAN JUAN DEL SU

C. K. GARRISON & CO
AGE

S. W. CORNER OF WASHINGTON AND BATTERY STS.
San Franci

IN A DISPUTE OVER THE CONTROL OF THE STEAMSHIP ROUTE
THROUGH NICARAGUA, WILLIAM WALKER MADE A FATAL MISTAKE
IN 1856 BY SIDING WITH C. K. GARRISON AND CHARLES MORGAN
AGAINST THE MIGHTY FINANCIER CORNELIUS VANDERBILT

Vanderbilt, now in complete control of the Accessory Transit Company, withdrew its steamers from service to Nicaragua and warned passengers not to travel across the dangerous Nicaraguan isthmus. He ordered all the transit company ships to be rerouted through Panama. Thus ended several years of successful operation of the Nicaraguan transit. The year 1855 had been its most prosperous one, but the intervention of William Walker, the Filibuster War, and the financial conflict involving Vanderbilt were to bring about its downfall.

The irate Commodore wrote a letter of protest to Secretary of State Marcy in Washington, suggesting that the State Department interfere in Nicaragua to protect the rights and property of U. S. citizens—such as Vanderbilt himself. He asked the United States government to take back from the aggressors (Morgan, Garrison, and Walker) their "plunder" (the transit company's property, worth about $1 million).

Vanderbilt found little support in the State Department, and none at all in the New York newspapers. After all, the press pointed out ironically, since the company was a Nicaraguan corporation, if Vanderbilt wanted relief he should apply to the Nicaraguan government itself (in other words, to William Walker).

Even though his Accessory Transit Company vessels were tied up in the ports of New York and San Francisco, the resourceful Vanderbilt knew full well that they had a nuisance value. The Pacific Mail Line was doing a tremendous business on the Panama route and wanted to avoid competition from the Commodore. Realizing his blackmail bargaining power, Vanderbilt agreed to keep his ships idle and not compete on the Panama route—if he were paid forty thousand dollars a month. His demands were met by the head of the Pacific Mail Line, and Vanderbilt, turning a loss into a gain, received several monthly payments.

By defying and antagonizing Vanderbilt, however, Walker had sown the seeds of his own destruction. The Accessory Transit Company could no longer bring him desperately needed supplies and fresh recruits, and Morgan and Garrison had not yet organized their own ships. Meanwhile, the other four Central American republics, as well as the Nicaraguan Legitimists, were preparing to attack Nicaragua to overthrow him. To make matters worse, Vanderbilt had managed to turn the conservative wing of the United States Congress against Walker.

The administration of Franklin Pierce observed Walker's activities in Nicaragua with increasing concern and hostility. Orders were sent to the principal port authorities to prevent unlawful military expeditions from leaving the United States, but it was difficult for U. S. officials to distinguish between filibuster volunteers and bona fide male passengers who wished to travel to Nicaragua. Despite regulations in United States ports to prevent it, during the previous six months Walker had received hundreds of recruits—posing as immigrants—for his army in Nicaragua.

FRANKLIN PIERCE
(1804–69)

Fourteenth president of the United States (1853–57). Issued a proclamation in 1854 against filibustering (fitting out armed expeditions to invade countries with which the United States was at peace). This decree hampered William Walker's activities on several occasions.

The Central American republics went on relentlessly with preparations to attack Walker. President Juan Rafael Mora of Costa Rica ordered up a large mobilization—three thousand Costa Rican troops—equipped with British arms, to fight the gringo invaders of Nicaragua. Ever since Walker had arrived in Central America, President Mora had been violently opposed to him, for it was evident that if Walker succeeded in Nicaragua, Costa Rica would probably be Americanized next. Great Britain helped Mora by supplying him with two thousand muskets equipped with improved sights and large supplies of ammunition.

The British government's interest in thwarting Walker was pointed out in an editorial in the *New York Sun* on May 16, 1856:

> For years the great aim of British policy in Central America has been to obtain a controlling influence in all the Central American States. England's aggressions in that quarter have been steadily pursued, with the view of strengthening her political power and bringing under her control the most available routes to the Pacific. She has robbed Honduras, intrigued in Guatemala, inflamed the envy and ambition of Costa Rica, dictated to Nicaragua, setting up pretensions to the Mosquito Coast, and seizing the only Nicaraguan port on the Atlantic side [Greytown], and now she is endeavoring by covert means [through the contribution of British arms and ammunition to Costa Rica] to crush the democratic party in Nicaragua, because that party has always expressed its preference for the United States.

(Ironically, if William Walker had been a British filibuster during the Victorian era, Britain probably would have supported his efforts vigorously instead of obstructing him.)

Although President Mora was undoubtedly a loyal and patriotic Central American, it is also true that Costa Rica was having a boundary dispute with Nicaragua involving the province of Guanacaste, and Mora didn't want a strong government in Nicaragua. Mora himself wished to gain control of the transit route and any future canal concessions for the benefit of Costa Rica. Furthermore, Mora was a Conservative and, like Great Britain, was opposed to the Liberal party that had invited Walker to Nicaragua in the first place.

PRESIDENT JUAN RAFAEL MORA OF COSTA RICA,
WHO DECLARED WAR AGAINST WILLIAM WALKER IN 1856
Mora was probably more instrumental in bringing about Walker's
ultimate defeat than any other Central American.

On March 1, 1856, President Mora declared war against the
Americans in Nicaragua. Walker immediately sent a battalion
of four companies, consisting of 240 men under the command
of Colonel Louis Schlessinger, to check this offensive threat.
Schlessinger was ordered to advance over the border to the
Costa Rican province of Guanacaste and surprise the enemy.
One of these filibuster companies was entirely French, a second
was all German. (It will be remembered that Schlessinger, a
linguist who spoke French, German, Spanish, and English, had
also fought with López in Cuba.)

Schlessinger was a capricious, hot-headed individualist,
totally unfit for military command. His troops were resentful;

en route to Costa Rica he forced them to march in the midday heat instead of during the cool of the night. He carelessly allowed his men to vault across streams, planting their rifles in the mud like poles and wetting the firearms' breeches instead of their own.

After a march of several days the filibusters reached the hacienda Santa Rosa, in Costa Rica itself, where Schlessinger decided to rest before advancing within Guanacaste. The hacienda's rustic and strongly constructed house was built on sloping land. Protected on two sides by solid stone walls, it seemed to be a veritable fortress. At least that was Schlessinger's opinion, so he didn't bother to scout the enemy territory or post guards.

Suddenly early in the afternoon of March 20 a number of

HACIENDA SANTA ROSA, COSTA RICA, SCENE OF A DISASTROUS DEFEAT OF THE FILIBUSTER ARMY, UNDER THE COMMAND OF COLONEL SCHLESSINGER, BY THE COSTA RICAN DEFENDERS

Costa Rican soldiers appeared on the slope in front of the hacienda's house and opened fire. The filibuster soldiers were enjoying a siesta, quite unprepared for battle. Schlessinger himself was frightened and bewildered. His troops were milling about, awaiting the orders of their commanding officer. Schlessinger peeked nervously around a corner of the house and, observing the enemy approaching up the hill, shouted in English: "There they are, boys!" Showing his linguistic talent as well as his speed of foot he then yelled in French over his shoulder: "Compagnie Française, garde-à-vous! Voici l'ennemi!" and in the German tongue: "Achtung! Hier kommt der Feind!" Thereupon he disappeared in the dense chaparral behind the hacienda's house, and that was the last anyone saw of Schlessinger for several days.

Following the discreet departure of their leader, most of the French and German troops threw down their muskets and beat a hasty retreat. Some heroic American officers attempted to make a stand and resist the onslaught of approximately five hundred Costa Rican soldiers, but in vain. The battle of Santa Rosa was over in about twenty minutes. Twenty of Schlessinger's men were killed and nineteen more taken prisoner by the enemy. President Mora ordered these prisoners, including the wounded, to be court-martialed immediately as armed invaders and shot. He published a decree in Spanish, English, French, and German to the effect that all filibusters captured while bearing arms would be executed, but those who surrendered to the Costa Rican army of their own free will would be pardoned.

About two weeks later Schlessinger appeared before William Walker and claimed that the defeat at Santa Rosa was due to lack of experience and slovenly discipline among his men. Other officers, however, who had witnessed the disastrous collapse disagreed: they unanimously charged Schlessinger himself with incompetence and cowardice. A court-martial was ordered, but before judgment could be passed Schlessinger deserted the filibuster army and fled to parts unknown. He was condemned to death in absentia, but was never captured by Walker.

VIRGIN BAY, NICARAGUA
Costa Rican troops killed ten unarmed United States employees of
the Transit Company and burned the company's wharves.

The victorious Costa Rican army, led by the president's
brother, General José Joaquín Mora, advanced into Nicaragua
and occupied the towns of Rivas and Virgin Bay. They gained
control for two months of the Transit Road, that twelve-mile
stretch damned by President Mora as the "highway of filibusterism." In Virgin Bay the Costa Ricans killed ten unarmed
employees of Vanderbilt's Accessory Transit Company, burned
the company's wharves and warehouses, and declared death to
all North Americans.

The shocking reverses at Santa Rosa and in Nicaragua weakened the morale in Walker's army. During the resulting panic
there were many desertions.

Meanwhile, in New York City "Nicaragua fever"—public
interest in Walker's exploits in Central America—was at its
height. A songwriter named Fred Shaw composed two comic
songs that were Broadway hits: "I'm Off for Nicaragua" (1856)
and "I've Been to Nicaragua" (1857). Selected lyrics from
these popular musical productions tell the story of a filibuster's
ups and downs:

El Nicaraguense.

OFFICIAL.

Court Martial of Colonel Louis Schlessinger.

GENERAL ORDERS—NO. 95.

HEADQUARTERS OF THE ARMY,
ADJUTANT GENERAL'S OFFICE.
Virgin Bay, May 3rd, 1856.

1. Before a General Court Martial convened by General Orders No. 73, and of which Brig. Gen. Goicouria, Departamente Intendencia General, is President, was arraigned and tried Col. Louis Schlessinger, 2d Rifles, N. A. on the following charges and specifications, viz:

Charge 1. Neglect of Duty.

Specification 1. In this, that Col. L. Schlessinger, N. A. did allow great confusion and disorder to exist in his command on the march from Virgin Bay to the Costa Rica frontiers, and did not exercise proper control over the officers and men of his command. All this on or about the 16th, 17th 18th 19th and 20th days of March, 1856.

Charge 2. Ignorance of his duties as a commanding officer.

AGENCY OF NICARAGUA
No. 347 Broadway.

The undersigned having been appointed by the government of Nicaragua, GENERAL EMIGRANT AGENT for that country in the United States has established a PERMANENT AGENCY, No. 347 Broadway, room No. 2, up stairs.

All persons desirous of obtaining information of any kind concerning Nicaragua will receive prompt attention by addressing the undersigned personally or by letter at the office of the Agency.

According to the Decree of the Nicaraguan Government dated Nov. 23, 1855, Emigrants are entitled to 250 acres of land, if single, and 350 acres are granted to families. The price of passage to Emigrants has been fixed at a very low figure, and for those will out means arrangements have been made with the Nicaraguan Emigration Company to advance the price of the passage upon the transfer of a part of the land granted by the Government.

This secures to Emigrants a LARGE GRANT OF LAND AND A FREE PASSAGE TO NICARAGUA.

DURING 1856 WILLIAM WALKER'S EMIGRANT AGENT IN NEW YORK LURED "COLONISTS" TO NICARAGUA THROUGH NEWSPAPER ADVERTISEMENTS

I'M OFF FOR NICARAGUA

Have you heard the way,
That's out to-day,
To better your Condition O;
Those who delight in,
Blood and fighting,
Join Walker's Expedition O—
There you can have all you can steal,
Without the chance of getting a meal,
Your names will live in books of story,
And you can live on Martial Glory.

Chorus: Then come along
And join the throng,
For victory and Walker, O;
Like a soldier gay,
I'll march away,
For "I'm off for Nicaragua O."

I'VE BEEN TO NICARAGUA

I.

One day while walking down Broadway,
What should I meet,
Coming up the street,
But a soldier gay,
In grand array,
Who had been to Nicaragua;
He took me warmly by the hand,
And says "old fellow" you're my man,
How would you like,
A soldier's life,
On the plains of Nicaragua?
Then come with me down to the ship,
I'll quickly send you, on your trip,
Don't stop to think, for there's meat and drink,
On the plains of Nicaragua.

II.

I scarcely knew what to do or say,
No money I had,
My boots was bad:
Hat was gone,
My pants were torn,
So I was off for Nicaragua;
He took me in, and did me treat,
Gave me a cigar, and grub to eat,
And on his scroll, did my name enrol,
A soldier for Nicaragua.

He took me down unto the ship,
Quickly sent me on my trip,
But, oh! lord, wasn't I sea-sick,
Going to Nicaragua.

III.

But after ten days of sailing away,
We saw the land, of San Juan,
Heart beat light,
For I thought it all right,
When I got to Nicaragua;
But when they got me on the shore,
They put me with about twenty more,
To fight away,
Or be hanged they say,
For going to Nicaragua.
Oh, wasn't I in a pretty fix,
If I could only have cut my sticks,
You'd never caught me playing such tricks,
As going to Nicaragua.

IV.

Next morning then in grand array,
All fagged and jaded,
We were paraded;
At close of day,
We were marched away,
To the Army in Nicaragua.
Not a bit of breakfast did I see,
And dinner was the same to me,
Two fried cats,
And three stewed rats,
Were supper in Nicaragua.
Marching all day with sore feet,
Plenty of fighting and nothing to eat,
How I sighed for pickled pigs' feet,
Way down in Nicaragua.

V.

The Costa-Ricans tackled us one day,
In the first alarm,
I lost my arm,
But we made them yield,
On Rivas field,
Way down in Nicaragua;
The Yankee boys fought long and well,
They gave those Costa Ricans fits,
But wasn't I dry,
And hun-ge-ry,

FILIBUSTERS FLAG IN NICARAGUA, 1856

The five points of the star represented the five Central American republics that William Walker planned to conquer in order to form a Central American slave empire with himself as dictator.

Way down in Nicaragua.
Marching all day, and fighting away,
Nothing to eat, quite as much pay,
Do it all for glory they say,
Way down in Nicaragua.

VI.

But when I was on duty one day
Give 'em the slip,
Jumped on the ship,
And bid good bye,
Forever, and Aye.
To the plains of Nicaragua.
And when I got to old New York,
I filled myself with Beans and Pork;
My friends I cheer, and in Lager Beer,
Drown times in Nicaragua.
And now I tread Columbia's land,
Take my friends all by the hand,
And if ever I leave 'em may I be—blessed,
To go to Nicaragua.

A ONE-WAY STEERAGE TICKET TO NICARAGUA FOR A RECRUIT
IN WILLIAM WALKER'S ARMY

William Walker in Nicaragua was obliged to concentrate on matters more serious than comic ditties. He set about regrouping his disorganized troops. He decided to eliminate companies of other nationalities and mustered all French and German recruits out of the filibuster army. The defeat at Santa Rosa caused considerable depression among Walker's officers, and many started to drink heavily to try to forget the disquieting military situation. The Filibuster cracked down hard on these groggy carousers, including his brother Norvell, whom he reduced in rank from captain to private.

A WARNING FROM WILLIAM WALKER

His officers in Nicaragua are ordered to set an example of temperance to the men under their command (probable date of issue December 1856):

"The commander-in-chief sees with regret that one of the chief military virtues—temperance—is not as much esteemed as it should be in the army. He earnestly exhorts the officers of the army to furnish in this respect an example of self-restraint and control to the men and to see properly punished socially as well as legally the intemperance which is calculated to bring the army into contempt and disgrace."

The demoralized troops were regrouped. With five hundred men Walker set out to attack Rivas, even though that town was occupied by three thousand of the enemy, mostly Costa Ricans. In this, the second battle of Rivas, both sides suffered heavy losses in street-by-street combat. After several hours of fierce fighting Walker's casualties in killed and wounded rose to about one-fourth his troops. It was estimated, however, that the Costa Ricans' losses were much more severe, with probably five of General Mora's soldiers falling for every filibuster.

SCENE IN THE BATTLE OF RIVAS, NICARAGUA

It was during this violent struggle that the national hero of Costa Rica, Juan Santamaría, courageously sacrificed his life. (The international airport at San José, Costa Rica, was named after him a century later.) Exposing himself to the deadly sniping of the filibusters, Santamaría, bearing a flaming torch,

STATUE OF THE COSTA RICAN
NATIONAL HERO,
JUAN SANTAMARIA, IN ALAJUELA,
COSTA RICA

This humble soldier is said to have sacrificed his life in April 1856 by setting fire to a house in Rivas, Nicaragua, held by William Walker and his officers. The international airport at San José, Costa Rica, has been renamed in Santamaria's memory.

ran across the street to the building where Walker and many Americans had taken refuge—and raising his arm set fire to the thatched roof of the gringos' stronghold. His mission accomplished, Santamaría died under a hail of bullets as the filibusters fled to safety in another building.

During the night Walker was forced to withdraw his dwindling forces from the town of Rivas. But this setback was countered by help from an unexpected quarter. In Rivas the bodies of the dead Costa Ricans were dumped into wells instead of being buried. As a result, an unseen ally—far stronger than any military weapon—suddenly came to William Walker's aid: cholera (acute infective enteritis) struck the bewildered Costa

JUAN SANTAMARIA
SETTING FIRE TO
WALKER'S HEAD-
QUARTERS DURING
THE BATTLE OF RIVAS

(From a painting by
Enrique Echandi.
Courtesy of
Henry M. Keith.)

Rican army, killing hundreds within a few days. This was in all probability the Asiatic cholera, now known as *Vibrio comma* (the rigid bacteria are shaped like commas), which was noted by medical writers in the Far East as early as the sixteenth century. An especially severe epidemic had taken place in India in 1850, spread westward to Europe in 1853, and was then carried by infected persons to North, Central, and South America. The appalling lack of sanitation among the Costa Rican troops in Rivas caused this horrible disease to make an explosive appearance. All severe outbreaks of cholera throughout history have been due to a contaminated public water supply, and such was the case at Rivas.

The disease-producing bacteria are spread by the ingestion of water and food contaminated by the excrement of the sick, the incubation period usually being two to three days. Cholera is characterized by copious vomiting, violent diarrhea, severe abdominal pains, intense thirst, and agonizing cramps of the legs, feet, and abdominal muscles. The surface of the body becomes blue or purple, the skin gets dry and wrinkled; the

NATIONAL (ANTI-WALKER) MONUMENT IN COSTA RICA In 1895 the Costa Ricans erected a dramatic bronze monument in the Parque Nacional, San José. It depicts the five angry, ravaged Central American republics driving away the defeated gringo filibuster, William Walker.

BATTLE OF RIVAS, NICARAGUA

pulse is extremely weak, there is complete suppression of urine, and the voice is reduced to a hoarse whisper. In untreated cases collapse and death can result in forty-eight hours, and during epidemics the fatality rate may average 50 percent.

The incidence of cholera today has been dramatically reduced in most parts of the world as a result of good sanitation, purification of drinking water, avoidance of uncooked vegetables, proper disposal of human excrement, and effectual quarantine methods, supplemented by the use of antibiotics—modern hygienic practices that were lacking or unknown at Rivas, Nicaragua, in April 1856.

The cholera precipitated a disorganized retreat from Rivas. General Mora himself returned hastily to Costa Rica, leaving his sick and dying troops in charge of his brother-in-law, José María Cañas. The dreaded *Vibrio* was carried back to Costa Rica, where it caused a frightful epidemic resulting in the deaths of at least ten thousand more victims among young and old, men, women, and children.

The cholera epidemic became so unbearable in Rivas that General Cañas, just before departing himself, wrote the following hasty letter to William Walker:

> Obliged to abandon Plaza of Rivas on account of the appearance of cholera in its most alarming form. I am forced to leave here a certain number of sick. . . . I expect your generosity will treat them with all the attention and care the situation requires. I invoke the laws of humanity in favor of these unfortunate victims of an awful calamity; and I have the honor to propose to you to exchange them, when they get well, for more than twenty of your prisoners who are now in our powers.

Instead of having them executed, as was the normal Central American military custom of the time, Walker immediately ordered his surgeons to take care of the sick Costa Ricans. His kind and humane treatment of the Costa Rican cholera victims won praise for the Filibuster in the United States and British newspapers. But public opinion in Central America was confused: if William Walker was "all bad," as people had been led to believe, how could he have a merciful side?

In May 1856 Walker received encouraging diplomatic news: Padre Agustín Vijil, the former curate of Granada who had been sent to Washington as minister to replace the unacceptable scoundrel Parker French, had been received formally by the State Department; the Nicaraguan government, at least for the time being, had been recognized by the United States.

Padre Vijil had been highly recommended to the State Department in Washington by U. S. minister John H. Wheeler, who described him as "a distinguished ornament of the church, of great learning and virtue." Provisional President Rivas of Nicaragua also praised Vijil as "a reliable person on account of his knowledge of public affairs and by his patriotic feelings."

Secretary of State Marcy might not have recognized Vijil if he had heard the padre's flowery sermon in Granada on October 29, 1855, when Vijil exclaimed: "Look at that man, General William Walker, sent by Providence to bring peace, prosperity, and happiness to this bloodstained, unhappy country."

In recognizing the Rivas government in Nicaragua, Secretary of State Marcy was in effect recognizing Walker's government, although he did not realize it at the time.

An editorial in a Northern newspaper gave a good picture of Padre Vijil:

> General Walker's Plenipotentiary, the Padre Vigil is just now the greatest lion in Washington. Happily for him, it is said he can't understand a word of English, so he will be saved the annoyance of hearing and reading all the remarks made about him. . . . As the correspondent of the *Evening Post* states that Padre Vigil had arrived in Washington *with his son,* his padreship must be something like General Pierce's soldiering, not of a kind to do any harm. The worst thing about the Padre is his unlucky name, which will of course, be the cause of a good many distressing puns: and small wits will be calling him a vigil-ant representative of Nicaragua, and so on. The Padre is represented as a rather stout, well-shaven man, whose long-skirted coat, knee-breeches, black hose and silver shoe-buckles accord with the priestly functions which he exercised at home. His hair is concealed by a sort of brown slouched cap.

Because of his close friendship with Walker, Padre Vijil was subjected to so much abuse, criticism, and ridicule by other Latin American foreign ministers in Washington that he soon resigned and departed in embarrassment.

PADRE AGUSTIN VIJIL
A Nicaraguan priest, sent by William Walker to Washington in May 1856 as his diplomatic representative. Vijil was provisionally recognized by the Pierce administration.

11

Walker "Elected" President of Nicaragua

IN JUNE 1856 a presidential "election" was held in Nicaragua. A few days prior to this election Walker and President Patricio Rivas had parted company, the last meeting between them taking place at León. The conversation was in Spanish, which Walker spoke with difficulty. "This country," said President Rivas, "is destroyed. You are seizing the power of the government and filling the offices of the state with unqualified men who have no knowledge of our language or our laws. We cannot allow your confiscation of estates. It only makes enemies. Peace with such a policy is impossible. You are no longer needed here. Your presence is harmful to us. The power which employed you originally and enlisted you in our cause can also depose you. It is necessary, señor general, that you disband your army and leave us."

"Pay my soldiers," Walker replied quietly but firmly.

"I will pay them in full," was the answer, "but you must leave the country. They shall all be paid, but every hostile American must depart at once."

Walker's face darkened and an expression of indescribable fierceness came over it. He advanced a step, drew his revolver, and shaking it slowly in the face of President Rivas, replied: "I remain and I govern, sir."

Patricio Rivas fled to Chinandega, where he joined the Central American allies against Walker. Rivas declared Walker to be a traitor and called upon all Nicaraguans between the ages of fifteen and sixty to fight against the Yankee invaders.

Walker accused Rivas of being a traitor himself, of having betrayed his country by inviting troops of Guatemala and El Salvador to invade Nicaragua. The Filibuster issued a decree abolishing Rivas's government and appointing Fermin Ferrer as provisional president of Nicaragua until elections could be held.

On Sunday, June 29, 1856, the "election" took place. When the votes were officially counted in Granada, William Walker had received almost sixteen thousand out of a total vote of approximately twenty-three thousand, thus becoming the new president of Nicaragua. *El Nicaraguense* claimed that the entire population took an interest in the election, and that it was the largest vote that had ever been polled in Nicaragua up to that time. Despite these claims by Walker's newspaper, there were undoubtedly many irregularities in the counting of the votes, and this election was a farce and a fraud.

WILLIAM WALKER WAS "ELECTED" PRESIDENT
OF NICARAGUA IN JUNE 1856
He established his presidential headquarters in Granada.

The truth of the matter was that by now Walker controlled only a small portion of the country; his Nicaraguan enemies held sway in León, Chinandega, and the vast central region of Nicaragua known as Matagalpa. Strong native Nicaraguan opposition prevented a fair election from being held country-wide; there was probably just some token voting in the areas controlled by Walker's army, such as Granada, Masaya, and Rivas. In any event, Walker was inaugurated on July 12, 1856.

Meanwhile, Secretary of State Marcy in Washington had authorized the United States minister in Nicaragua, John H. Wheeler, to establish diplomatic relations with the Nicaraguan government, little dreaming that the new president would be William Walker. Minister Wheeler, known in Nicaragua as *el ministro filibustero*, gave a prompt but broad interpretation to the instructions from Washington and hastily recognized Walker. Wheeler was not impartial. As a plantation owner and slaveholder in the South he was a staunch advocate of white

JOHN H. WHEELER
Wheeler, United States minister to Nicaragua in 1856, was known as "El Ministro Filibustero." Secretary of State Marcy reprimanded and recalled Wheeler for being too friendly toward William Walker.

WILLIAM L. MARCY
Secretary of state (1853–
1857). Marcy strongly
opposed William Walker,
whom he considered an
outlaw.

supremacy. He endorsed Walker's supposition that the United States should annex territories in Central America and the Caribbean to guide the nations of those areas to decent government and a better life. In his memoirs Wheeler asserted that "the race of Central Americans have conclusively proved to all observant minds that they are incapable of self-government."

When Secretary of State Marcy in Washington became aware of the happenings in Nicaragua two months later, the United States abruptly withdrew recognition of Walker's government. Wheeler was called back to Washington and severely reprimanded for his undiplomatic conduct in overtly favoring Walker and interfering in the internal affairs of Nicaragua. Wheeler was forced to resign.

William Walker's inauguration as president of Nicaragua took place in the main plaza in Granada at eleven o'clock on the morning of July 12, 1856, with much ceremonial pomp and a parade led by "Uncle Billy" (as Walker's troops affectionately called him) on a white horse. Companies of soldiers marched briskly in step as the band played "Yankee Doodle," "Hail, Columbia," and "Oh! Susanna." Colorful flags and abundant flowers formed a brilliant background for the Filibuster as he ascended the speaker's platform. The cheering multitude (or at least some admirers) shouted "Viva el Presidente!" Walker did in fact still enjoy some support from poor young men of military age because he had abolished the highly unpopular forced military service in Nicaragua.

The new president's drab and undersized figure must have been disappointing to the excited crowd. He was dressed in a shabby black coat, a flannel shirt, baggy trousers, and a rather old felt hat. A reporter from the *New York Tribune* wrote that Walker looked like a "grocery keeper from one of the poorer localities of the Sixth Ward."

Thirteen months after arriving in Nicaragua with fifty-eight soldiers of fortune William Walker became the de jure ruler of the country. On bended knee, he swore to govern justly the free republic of Nicaragua for a period of two years.

Walker, the Anglo-Saxon imperialist, delivered his inaugural speech in English, followed by Colonel Lainé, his Cuban aide, reading the address in Spanish. According to *El Nicaraguense* of July 19, 1856, Walker spoke in a clear, firm, confident tone. It had been rumored that he would take advantage of the occasion to seek to annex Nicaragua to the United States, but in his address he warned the great powers, both nearby and distant, that Nicaragua intended to control her own destiny at any cost:

> In our relations with the more powerful nations of the world, I hope they may be led to perceive that although Nicaragua may be comparatively weak, she is yet jealous of her honor, and determined to maintain the dignity of her independent sovereignty. Her geographical position and commercial advantages may attract the cupidity of other governments, either neighboring or distant, but, I trust, they may yet learn

that Nicaragua claims to control her own destiny. . . . The greatest possible freedom of trade will be established, with the view of making Nicaragua what Nature intended her to be—the highway for commerce between two oceans.

After he finished his speech, the cheering was said to have been "spontaneous and almost deafening."

The Filibuster seemed to be on the way to accomplishing a grandiose mission: establishing a powerful slave empire in Central America, with himself as dictator. The strategic geographical position and abundant natural resources of Nicaragua made the country a prize worthy of the attention of the United States, England, France, and Spain.

William Walker was in all likelihood the second native-born American to become president of a foreign country; ironically, the first was Joseph Jenkins Roberts, a Virginia-born freeman of Negro ancestry, who in 1847 was elected president of the new independent republic of Liberia.

Walker's bizarre success in Nicaragua brought various reactions. Throughout Latin America it caused fear and consternation. Repercussions were felt as far south as Chile, where in 1856 a conference took place to discuss the protection of South America from a possible future attack by William Walker and his gringo filibusters. But Walker's triumph was celebrated at Purdy's National Theatre in New York City in late July 1856. A popular drama entitled "Nicaragua, or General Walker's Victories" was presented.

The action of the play took place in Granada and Rivas. The attack on Granada, scenes of street fighting, prison romance, and Spanish dances were offered. The musical numbers featured a medley—"Filibuster Overture"—and the song "I Won't Die an Old Maid." A large cast included "General Walker, the hope of Freedom," "Jefferson Squash, a roving Yankee," "Hans Pikeltuhb, a dealer in Schnapps," "Cranbery Cockles, a conceited Cockney," "General Mora, President of Costa Rica," and "Ivory Black, a superior Nigger." The producers of this extravaganza were capitalizing on Walker's incredible audacity and national fame, on his appeal to believers in Manifest Destiny even in the North.

Meanwhile, back in Nicaragua, Walker needed money. During September 1856 various decrees were passed to obtain funds for the new Nicaraguan government and encourage immigration by North Americans. Court proceedings were permitted to be held in either Spanish or English. Since all legal transactions in Nicaragua were normally conducted in Spanish, the use of English favored North Americans. The estates of Walker's political enemies were confiscated to be sold at public auction. Payments could be made either in United States dollars or Nicaraguan scrip. A $500,000 twenty-year loan at 6 percent interest was authorized, to be secured by one million acres of Nicaraguan public land.

Instrumental in promoting this loan and promulgating subsequent decrees to be issued by Walker was Pierre Soulé, a Frenchman who had settled in New Orleans and had subsequently become a lawyer, U. S. senator, and U. S. minister to Spain. Soulé was more ardently proslavery than the most fervent native-born Southerner. He had been the principal architect of the 1854 Ostend Manifesto, which, it will be remembered, strongly implied that if Spain refused to sell Cuba, then the United States should go to war to wrest the island from Spain by force.

Soulé seems to have exerted a very strong influence on Walker's thinking. Although the Filibuster had been born in Tennessee, as a journalist on the *Daily Crescent* in New Orleans he had generally opposed the proslavery faction of the Democratic party. Now, however, needing the wholehearted support of the solid South, Walker decided to follow Soulé's zealous advice and reinstitute involuntary labor in Nicaragua.

Since the native Nicaraguans were too easygoing to meet American work standards, very strict antilabor laws were passed, punishing vagrancy and establishing a system of veritable peonage for Nicaraguan laborers. Walker's most far-reaching decree authorized the reintroduction of African slavery to Nicaragua (where it had been abolished in 1824), in order to "regenerate" the country.

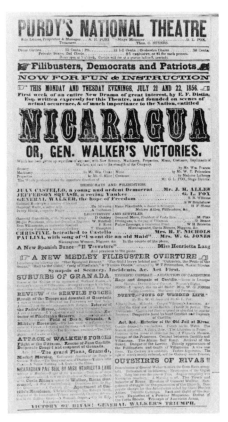

Forrest Theater!

O. E. BINGHAM, ... MANAGER

THE INIMITABLE **MISS**

ALBERTINE!

THE CELEBRATED AMERICAN ACTRESS,

Will appear as

BESS, the Nightingale of the Army

And by particular desire, in her favorite Character of

BOB NETTLES!

The Grand Nicaraguan Drama of The

SIEGE of GRENADA

Having been highly successful in every continued Scene, will be repeated to-night.

TUESDAY EVENING, JUNE 16, 1857,

Will be presented (2d time in Sacramento) the thrilling Drama of

THE SIEGE
—OF—
GRENADA!

Or, WALKER AND HIS MEN!

Gen. Walker, President of the Republic of Nicaragua ......Mr. MORTIMER
Gen. Henningson, Commander American Forces in Nicaragua, J. R. PAULLIN
Col. O'Nell, his Aid-de-Camp .... ROGERS
Col. Henry, Acting Quarter Master General, ... JACKSON
Lieut. Ben O'Neil, brother of the Col. .... Miss CARPENTER
Pat. Kenoran, a Brock of a Boy .... DUMPHRIES
Arkansaw, half horse—half alligator .... McGOWAN
Jack of St. Giles, ... POTTER
Negro Pete, ... AUSTIN
Ned, ... **Mr. O. E. BINGHAM**
Bess, Ned's Wife, the Nightingale of the Nicaraguan Army,
Miss ALBERTINE
Ethel, Florence, Jenny and Julien—Ned and Elizabeth's children—Little Rose
Bingham, Little Francis, Julia and James.

SPANIARDS:

Gen'l Beloss, Commander-in-Chief of Native forces,........... DENNIS
Price, an American in Spanish pay, ... FERGUSON
Soldiers, Emigrants, Spies, &c. by numerous auxilliaries.

ACT 1.—SCENE 1. Onward is the beacon light of Liberty! Behind is the
dark gulf of tyranny.
SCENE 2. Four thousand of the enemy surrounding the town—The Charge!
Come on! brothers.
SCENE 3. Bess—I can, at least, load your rifle for you.
SCENE 4. No quarters! FIRE!

IN JULY 1856 A MUSICAL COMEDY WAS PRESENTED AT PURDY'S THEATRE IN NEW YORK CITY, CELEBRATING GENERAL WILLIAM WALKER'S VICTORIES IN NICARAGUA

ANOTHER AMERICAN THEATRICAL PERFORMANCE CONCERNING WILLIAM WALKER
In June 1857 the Forrest Theater in Sacramento, California, presented the drama "Siege of Granada, or, Walker and His Men."

Naturally, William Walker enjoyed considerable favorable publicity in the South as a standard-bearer for the doctrine of Manifest Destiny. A Virginian named Hofer, writing in the expansionist and proslavery *De Bow's Review* of August 1856, commented:

It is immaterial whether Walker succeeds in Nicaragua to establish himself or whether he succumbs to the powers that are brought to bear against him. Nature will have its way and Walker . . . is but the precursor of a mightier power, an evolutionary instrument in the hands of an unchangeable fate. . . . We believe, and believe firmly, in the destiny of our country as made manifest by the spirit of American propagandism and the genius of the American people.

PIERRE SOULE
Jurist and politician, born in France but settled in New Orleans and became a very ardent proslavery jingoist. Soulé persuaded William Walker in 1856 to pass a decree authorizing the reintroduction of African slavery to Nicaragua.

Down in Nicaragua, events beyond Walker's control caused his extraordinary proclamation on slavery to be pigeonholed. Before new planters and slaves could be brought to Nicaragua, the remaining four Central American republics would have to be conquered, or at least subdued. By this time both parties in Nicaragua had turned against Walker, to be added to his long list of enemies—among them Cornelius Vanderbilt, Great Britain, and the Northern states of the United States. Even his erstwhile friend and loyal supporter Colonel Mariano Mendez changed sides, moved to León to join the Central American allies, and denounced the Filibuster. Mendez issued a proclamation to Nicaraguans and all Central Americans that fervently summarized anti-Walker sentiment:

COMPATRIOTS: A foreign tyrant, far more fatal than the Spanish conquerors, has appeared among us: William Walker has committed the fearful crime of rising against the supreme government of the republic, setting up for himself alone to sanction the foreignization of the territory of our native land, the extinction of our religion, and the perpetual slavery of our race. Shall we with cool indifference gaze upon this tremendous crime? Certainly not. Die before seeing the fate of the

nation in the hands of a foreign traitor. The cause is holy, very holy.
It is the cause of our fatherland; it is the cause of our religion; it is the
cause of our liberty. To die, therefore, for such sublime objects is
glorious and grand for a truly republican heart; and I, appreciating
and loving these sentiments, swear before God and society that I will
sacrifice all that is most dear to defend rights so sacred, and I will
irrigate the tree of liberty with my blood.

Mariano Mendez

Opposed by so many enemies, Walker would not only have
to increase the size of his army, but also organize a navy. In
July 1856 a Costa Rican schooner, the *San José* was seized at
San Juan del Sur, expropriated from its owner, Mariano Salazar,
and rechristened the *Granada*. Salazar, a wealthy Nicaraguan
merchant, prominent army officer, and Democratic politician,
had been friendly with Walker at first. There had subsequently

WALKER'S ONE-SHIP NAVY WON A BATTLE
The puny filibuster schooner "Granada" managed to sink the larger
Costa Rican warship "Once de Abril" near San Juan del Sur in
November 1856.

been friction between them, however, when the Filibuster objected to a shady deal in which Salazar had sold a large quantity of Brazil-wood timber to the Nicaraguan government at an inflated price in order to make an exorbitant profit for himself. To punish him for this transgression, Walker jailed Salazar for a few hours in the prison at León, until local politicians explained it was nothing to get excited about—merely the usual way of doing business with the government.

Salazar was infuriated over this incident; he started to intrigue against Walker while openly slandering and vilifying the Americans in Nicaragua.

CAPTAIN CALLENDER I. FAYSSOUX

Born in Missouri, Fayssoux served as a midshipman in the Texas navy; subsequently he accompanied Narciso López on two disastrous filibustering expeditions to Cuba before becoming commander of William Walker's navy in Nicaragua.

A LETTER OF SYMPATHY

Many of William Walker's soldiers died of "fevers" contracted in Nicaragua (including both of his brothers, Norvell and James). This letter of sympathy, which shows the compassionate side of Walker, was written by him to the widow of a filibuster, William Hamilton Bowie, who died in Granada, Nicaragua, in September 1856:

Granada Oct. 1st, 1856

My dear Madam:

It is my painful duty to inform you of the death of Mr. Bowie. Soon after he arrived here he was attacked by the fever; and he was just recovering from the effects of this attack when he was taken down with an acute inflammation of the stomach and bowels, of which he died.

I know, Madam, that it is useless to offer condolence in such a bereavement. I well know that nothing can console you for the loss of a husband of such noble and generous qualities as was Mr. Bowie. Still I beg leave to sympathize with you in your affliction; and if there is aught I can do to render your loss less heavy and insupportable, you have but to command me.

Mr. Bowie was dear to me as a friend and if there is any way in which I can be of service to you I hope you will not deny me the mournful pleasure of rendering some small tribute to his memory.

With deep sympathy,
I remain, Madam,
Your Obedient servant,
Wm. Walker

to Mrs. H. Bowie

The *Granada,* converted to a schooner-of-war, was placed under the command of Lieutenant Callender Fayssoux from Missouri, a veteran filibuster and strict disciplinarian who had served with Narciso López in Cuba. As luck would have it, one of Fayssoux's first naval accomplishments was to capture Mariano Salazar in a *bungo* or small flatboat out on the Gulf of Fonseca. Salazar had in his possession some incriminating anti-American letters. He was dispatched to Granada under guard, accused of treason by Walker, and condemned to death. This unfortunate Nicaraguan was executed by a firing squad on the plaza at Granada on Sunday afternoon August 3, 1856.

In November 1856 the *Granada,* with two six-pound guns and a crew of twenty-eight, engaged in combat the larger Costa Rican brig *Once de Abril,* which possessed far superior gunpower and a complement of nearly one hundred. In a two-hour sea fight Fayssoux managed to outmaneuver the Costa Ricans and sink the *Once de Abril,* rescuing forty-one survivors. From the beach at San Juan del Sur the fire and explosion of this sea battle was witnessed by spectators, who could hardly believe that the *Granada* had won the day. Walker promoted Fayssoux to the rank of captain in the one-ship filibuster "navy," and presented him with the valuable hacienda Rosario, near Rivas, as a fitting reward for his maritime victory.

On land, however, things were beginning to go badly for Walker. The Filibuster had a theory about how to wage war in Central America:

> The best manner of treating a revolutionary movement . . . is to treat it as a boil, let it come to a head, and then lance it, letting all the bad matter out at once. A war against scattered guerillas is more exhausting than a contest with the enemy gathered in masses.

It would soon be tested.

12

The Tide Turns

TOWARD the end of 1856 Walker was being attacked on several fronts by a combined Central American alliance consisting of Costa Rica (under General José Joaquín Mora), Guatemala (under General José Victor Zavala), Honduras (under General Florencio Xatruch), El Salvador (under General Ramón Belloso), and Nicaragua itself under the command of Generals Tomás Martínez, Máximo Jerez, and José Dolores Estrada. The numbers of Central American allied troops were increasing far more rapidly than were Walker's beleaguered forces.

Perhaps the most astute of these attacking Central American generals was General Zavala of Guatemala. Witty and talkative, he was curious about the personality of William Walker. On one occasion, during an exchange of prisoners, he queried Lieutenant Livy Lewis, a representative of the Filibuster:

"Does General Walker smoke?" The answer was no.
"Does General Walker gamble?" "No, sir," replied Lewis.
"Does General Walker drink?" The answer was also no.
"Does General Walker have any mistresses?"
"No, sir," answered Lewis. "He has no vices we know about. Why does the General ask these questions?"

General Zavala replied that if Walker didn't smoke, didn't gamble, didn't drink, and wasn't interested in women, it was apparent that he wanted and loved only one thing: the sensuality of power; and for this reason he had become a filibuster. General Zavala then added frankly that he didn't trust a man who didn't enjoy at least some vices.

The facetious Zavala's sarcastic witticisms sometimes irritated his fellow Central American leaders. For example, he dubbed the vacillating General Belloso of El Salvador "Nana" (meaning "nursemaid"); Patricio Rivas, the former provisional president of Nicaragua who had turned against Walker and joined the allies, he derisively nicknamed "Patas Arriba" ("Upside Down"). It has been suggested that without the constant bickering among their generals, the Central American allied troops could have conquered Walker much sooner.

GENERAL J. VICTOR ZAVALA
Known is his youth as the "D'Artagnan of Guatemala," led the Guatemalan troops who fought against William Walker in Nicaragua (after General Mariano Paredes died of cholera).

For Nicaragua, the most important battle of the war against the filibusters took place at San Jacinto in September 1856. This battle is commemorated and celebrated by Nicaraguans, since it was a contest where all-Nicaraguan troops fought against and defeated all-American forces. The Nicaraguans had their own local hero in this struggle—a first sergeant named Andrés Castro, who, when his carbine failed to fire, stood up and killed a filibuster with a rock. The battle of San Jacinto lifted the morale of the Central American allies and encouraged them to attack Walker, instead of waiting for him. Walker suffered an additional blow at San Jacinto: his friend and adviser Byron Cole (probably the kindest and gentlest of the filibusters) was caught by a detachment of Nicaraguan troops and hanged.

ON THE LEFT, ONE OF THE ANTIQUATED MUSKETS USED BY THE NICARAGUAN ARMY THAT FOUGHT AGAINST WALKER AT THE BATTLE OF SAN JACINTO IN SEPTEMBER 1856; ON THE RIGHT, A LONGER AND MORE EFFECTIVE RIFLE USED BY THE YANKEE FILIBUSTERS

NICARAGUAN HERO ANDRES CASTRO, WHO, WHEN HIS CARBINE FAILED, KILLED A GRINGO FILIBUSTER WITH A ROCK IN THE BATTLE OF SAN JACINTO, SEPTEMBER 1856

A LATIN AMERICAN ARTIST'S PORTRAYAL OF THE BATTLE OF
SAN JACINTO, IN WHICH NICARAGUAN TROOPS DEFEATED THE
FILIBUSTER ARMY OF WILLIAM WALKER

At this point, Walker received some valuable aid from an
unexpected source: Charles Frederick Henningsen, a noted
European soldier of fortune, became interested in his cause.
Henningsen, a veritable military genius, was born in England
in 1818 of Swedish parents. By the time he was twenty he had
obtained the rank of full colonel in the Carlist army in Spain
as the result of gallantry in combat. Following a period of
service in the Russian army, he turned up in Hungary, where
he won further laurels for military strategy in the losing battle
for independence. He followed the Hungarian patriot Lajos
Kossuth to the United States.

Henningsen's luck turned for the better when he met a charming, rich widow from Georgia, whom he married. Making use
of his considerable literary talent, he dashed off some personal
memoirs about his hazardous experiences in Russia and Hungary. He then devoted his attention to the improvement of
weapons, assembling the first Minié rifles ever manufactured
in the United States.

Henningsen had war in his blood, and upon hearing that William Walker was in desperate need of an experienced military strategist in Central America, he left immediately for Nicaragua without much urging. He brought down with him some newfangled mortars, howitzers, and a considerable supply of rifles and ammunition, supplied in part by the bountiful generosity of Mrs. Henningsen.

Walker promptly commissioned Henningsen a brigadier general, made him second in command, and put his military knowledge to the test. It was a critical period for the Filibuster, who was attempting to wage a war on two fronts with only six hundred men. The gringo army was succumbing to cholera, typhus, yellow fever, and amoebic dysentery at an alarming rate. Food was growing scarce, desertions were increasing.

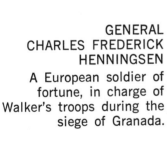

GENERAL CHARLES FREDERICK HENNINGSEN
A European soldier of fortune, in charge of Walker's troops during the siege of Granada.

By the time of Henningsen's arrival in Nicaragua, Walker had established his military headquarters at Granada. The Central American allies were massing some three thousand troops in the strongly fortified town of Masaya, about twelve miles to the northwest.

In November 1856 Walker boldly decided to attack Masaya with three hundred men, hoping that with the aid of Henningsen's unusual new mortars he could force the surrender of the entire allied army. During three days of ceaseless fighting, Masaya was assaulted—but to no avail. The fuses of the unfamiliar mortars were poorly timed, causing the shells to explode harmlessly in the air instead of on the ground. The numerically superior enemy controlled the principal streets of Masaya with withering cross fire. Night and day, deafened by a ceaseless roar of musketry, the Americans smashed and cut their way through the inside walls of a long row of houses leading to the main plaza, house by house. There was no time for meals other than a hastily snatched piece of hardtack; the incessant din of battle made sleep impossible. When the embattled filibusters got within thirty yards of the plaza they had to abandon the attack, owing to sheer physical exhaustion and crippling losses—a third of their number had been killed or wounded. The surviving Americans withdrew under the cover of darkness and wearily retreated to Granada, where more adversity awaited them.

Granada, the traditional Legitimist capital, stood on a gently sloping plain near the shores of Lake Nicaragua. The oldest Spanish colonial city in Nicaragua, it had been founded in 1524 by Francisco Hernandez de Córdoba. During the sixteenth and seventeenth centuries it was a major port for Spanish colonial trade, in direct contact with Cadiz and Seville, until a strong earthquake in the late 1600s caused shallows to develop in the San Juan River and curtailed galleon traffic. Its houses reflected typical Spanish-American architectural style: the larger homes of the wealthy were constructed of stone, adobe brick, and cement, usually one story high, with a stern, forbidding exterior, including heavily barred windows and a

WEARY RETREAT OF WALKER'S SOLDIERS AFTER LOSING THE
BATTLE OF MASAYA TO NICARAGUAN TROOPS

massive wooden door. From the outside one would never
imagine how attractive the interior patio could be, possibly
with a charming fountain in its center, surrounded by shady
open corridors and embellished by flowering plants. The high
ceilings of the spacious interior rooms kept them pleasantly
cool, even during the intense midday heat.

This beautiful cradle of the Legitimist party gradually turned
into a pesthole. The Central American allies descended upon
Granada en masse, surrounded it, and assaulted it from three
sides. Lack of hygiene caused appalling sickness among
Walker's trapped and beleaguered troops, constantly under
enemy attack.

Harper's Weekly gave a vivid description of the conditions
the filibuster army underwent during the siege:

> There was no clean linen for the sufferers, and they had to lie in their
> filthy woolen clothes, which had served for months as a uniform by day
> and as pajamas at night. The cots were never cleaned or fumigated,
> and a wounded man would probably be assigned to a dingy one upon
> which some wretch a few hours before had succumbed to fever or
> cholera. Flies swarmed over festering wounds and transmitted infec-

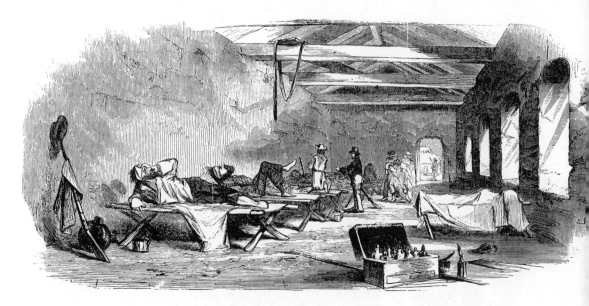

THE HOSPITAL AT GRANADA, NICARAGUA

tion from one patient to another. Vermin crawled over the bodies and
in the hair of the sufferers. Many cried in vain for water; others were
raving with delirium and would sometimes roll from their cots and lie
for hours on a filthy floor before being replaced by incompetent at-
tendants. The odor was almost overpowering, even to the strong and
well. Worst of all, each day the places gave forth an array of ghastly
corpses. It is not remarkable that in the presence of such depressing
scenes the Americans were prone to resort to hard drinking, and that
to the epidemics of fever and cholera there was added a third—desertion. When conditions were at their worst the daily mortality amounted
to two or three per cent of the total American population, and at the
time Granada was evacuated the death rate was so high that the surgeons declared that unless there were a change for the better every
American in Nicaragua would be dead within six weeks.

Before the allies attacked, Walker decided to move some two
hundred of his own sick and wounded from Granada across the
lake to the volcanic island of Ometepe, where many died from
exposure. In the meantime, hundreds of shocked, miserable
Granadans streamed out of their city through the allied lines
to seek refuge in Masaya and various nearby villages.

The filibuster leader left Henningsen with orders to destroy
Granada, since it could no longer be defended. Henningsen
organized his men into demolition squads and proceeded to
blow up and burn the Legitimist capital block by block. For
seventeen days, while fighting off repeated attacks by the
enemy, the Americans annihilated building after building in a

STREET SCENE IN GRANADA,
NICARAGUA

PIER BUILT BY ORDER
OF GENERAL WALKER
ON LAKE NICARAGUA,
AT GRANADA

VIEW OF GRANADA, NICARAGUA, FROM THE WEST, 1854

frenzied orgy of fire and drink. Many homes were so well stocked with wines, aguardiente, and other liquor that some filibusters were intoxicated for the entire seventeen days. So much strong drink was available that Henningsen's men poured it down their throats like thirsty travelers drinking at a spring in the desert. Subsequently a reporter in Panama queried an American officer who had survived the horrors of the protracted siege: "Why did you allow yourselves to be so badly cornered in Granada?" "The truth is," he replied, "we were all drunk."

At nightfall flames shot skyward and clouds of smoke settled on the rooftops, as the howling, drunken filibusters wallowed in destruction and plunder. Henningsen set fire to the buildings on the main plaza and captured the church of Guadalupe. In this substantial stone place of worship some four hundred men, women, and children were crowded together, at least half of whom were sick or wounded.

When the enemy sent a letter to Henningsen, calling upon him to surrender and offering the filibusters protection and free transportation out of the country, Henningsen sent a defiant reply.

The Central American allies, although suffering heavy losses, were constantly receiving reinforcements, while sickness, wounds, death, and desertions were decimating the ranks of the Americans. Henningsen never seemed to rest as he comforted the wounded and exhorted the groggy filibusters to continue the struggle. When supplies of ammunition dwindled, an ingenious officer named Swingle made improvised cannonballs out of iron scraps, clay, and molten lead.

The head nurse in the church was Mrs. Edward Bingham, a Florence Nightingale who selflessly cared for the sick and wounded day and night—until she herself collapsed and died of cholera. Her husband, an invalid actor who had come to Nicaragua to accept one of Walker's land grants and seek a peaceful life, somehow survived the siege and eventually made his way to California. On February 7, 1857, the *New-York Daily Times* paid tribute to Mrs. Bingham in an article entitled "A Florence Nightingale in Walker's Camp":

LANDING HOSPITAL PATIENTS
FOLLOWING THE EVACUATION
OF GRANADA

Two years ago an actor, named Bingham, was shot in the city of Panama. From the effect of this shot Bingham was laid up, in Panama, for about seven weeks, and completely lost the use of his lower limbs: nor has he at any time since been able to walk. Recovering sufficiently to be moved, he came on to New York, physically helpless, and completely destitute of funds.

His wife, who was playing at some provincial theatre, now heard of the arrival of her husand, and, as soon as possible, joined him. Mrs. Bingham procured employment at the Bowery Theatre, and endeavored to support her husband and three children, all of whom were entirely dependent on her exertions. After struggling in this way for some months, the Bowery Theatre was closed, and with it her only means of sustenance. During the past year, Bingham and his family occupied wretched apartments in a tenement-house in Stanton Street, and, after the theatrical resource failed, were obliged to rely for subsistence on the voluntary contributions of friends and public charity. In August last, Mrs. Bingham was confined. Deprived of her assistance, the family was almost reduced to starvation. Frequently, Mr. Bingham relates, he passed thirty-six and forty-eight hours without tasting a morsel of food, and knew of no source from which relief would come. The Baptist Society in Stanton Street contributed something to their support, and a trifling aid came from members of his own profession. Two of the children, boys, aged eight and ten years, were taken by the proprietor of a traveling circus, who agreed to support them for their services, such as they might be.

The mother at length became well enough to go out, and spent several days in the futile attempt to procure work. At length when the hope of bearing up against misfortune was almost exhausted, she came across the advertisement of the Nicaraguan Agency, which offered to every emigrant who would go to Nicaragua a free passage and a certain number of acres of land. Mr. Bingham being well enough in body, except that his lower limbs were useless, and thinking he could teach school or otherwise employ himself in Nicaragua—that, at all events, he was no more likely to starve there than here, concluded to take his family thither as soon as possible. . . .

From the time of her arrival Mrs. Bingham has occupied herself with attending to the sick and the wounded of General Walker's army, braving all the perils of camp diseases, everywhere bestowing on the invalid soldiers such kind attentions and careful treatments as to elicit the deepest gratitude and the most friendly regard. But her brave devotion in the hospitals proved fatal to herself at length—the intelligence arriving by the last steamer that she had sickened from the prevalent fever and died (at Granada).

Finally Walker, who had been out on the lake awaiting reinforcements, came to rescue Henningsen from the smoky bedlam with some fresh recruits from New Orleans and San Francisco. The surviving Americans had to fight their way, foot by foot, down the street that led to the wharf on Lake Nicaragua. Only 111 overtired filibusters survived to stagger out of the smoldering ruins. As he was leaving this scene of utter desolation, Henningsen, with a flair for the dramatic, hung a sign on a charred lance: the written reminder that "Aquí fué Granada" (Granada was here).

The most shameful and tragic siege in Central American history had ended. The wanton destruction of Granada by the Americans was a ruthless act of vandalism and spite. William Walker asserted later that for strategic reasons he wanted to prevent his enemies from capturing an important, renowned stronghold. As it turned out, he incurred the hostility of all Central America through this barbaric and seemingly needless demolition of a cherished metropolis.

In December 1856 a young drummer boy who had escaped from duty in General Walker's army in Nicaragua arrived in New York City on the S. S. Tennessee. He gave the following straightforward account of his military experiences, as recorded by a reporter of the *New-York Daily Times* at the Quarantine Hospital on Staten Island:

Young Acker was sitting close to a hot stove, evidently trying to recover from the effects of the atmosphere which had pierced his attenuated form. His whole appearance gave evidence of the hardships and suffering through which he has passed, and excited emotions of pity and commiseration for his youth and his misfortunes. His flesh was wasted, and his countenance cadaverous and haggard from disease and want, and his wardrobe altogether too scanty for the rigors of the season. Young Acker possesses an intelligent face and mild and pleasing eye. We give his narrative very much in his own words, as it was delivered in answer to questions put to him: "My name is ROBERT ACKER; I am a native of New York City, and fifteen years old; my father and mother are dead; I have a brother living in the City; I was a drummer in Gen. WALKER's army; learned to drum with a boy in Williamsburg; left New York in the steamer *Tennessee,* about three months ago; I had been driving a milk wagon in the City, and was told by the men who were getting recruits for Gen. WALKER that boys could get three dollars a day there, and men five and six dollars; a free passage was offered me to Nicaragua, and when we were all together there were about 250; they were mostly New York boys and from the ages of fifteen to thirty— rather hard cases; they were mostly drunk when they came on board, and drank all they could get on the passage; I do not drink; on the steamer we were fed on salt beef and pork, potatoes, hard bread and coffee, and were well enough satisfied with the fare.

THE FILIBUSTERS WERE HARASSED BY CHOLERA, MALARIA, DYSENTERY, AND CENTRAL AMERICAN LICE

"Upon landing at San Juan we proceeded up the river in a flat-boat to General WALKER's head-quarters at Granada; we arrived late in the evening of the second day, and General WALKER came out and reviewed us the same night; I was then in good health, and pleased with the appearance of the country and things in general; we found the troops living in the native houses, which were used as barracks; the houses are built of turf, (adobes,) of one story, and covered with tiles; they were comfortable; there were about nine hundred at Granada, including our company, and exclusive of natives about the camp; I saw General WALKER frequently busy among his troops.

"During the six weeks we remained at Granada, about thirty of our company died, mostly of chills and fever; *and at the end of three months, nearly all our company had died;* they did not drink much, for though there was plenty of *aguardiente,* they had no money to pay for it. The food served to the soldiers at Granada was fresh beef and coffee; we had no salt or bread; I could eat but little of it, and would go hungry till I could stand it no longer, and then try it again; the men soon became weakened by their fare and by sickness, and seemed discouraged at the prospects before them.

"The first battle was at León, about a day's journey from Granada. The forces, about one thousand strong, started at 10 o'clock in the morning, under General WALKER, and arrived about 7 in the evening. I went ahead as drummer, and there was another behind; this was all the music we had. We laid down in the grass, when we got to León, and in about half an hour the enemy charged upon us, before we had fired a gun, but as we rose up they 'left.' Col. MARKAM was with the forces. The next morning they charged on us again; we fired a shell into their ranks when they were about an eighth of a mile off, and when the smoke of the guns had cleared away there was none of the enemy in sight; another shot was fired, and the rifles rushed in and took possession of the small plaza; General HORNSBY then, with the infantry, went to the large plaza, but after firing a few shots retreated; the enemy took possession of the houses and fired upon our troops until 1 o'clock in the morning, when they vacated the town and went to Granada. At 2 o'clock our forces started after them, and on the way we met four hundred of the enemy who, on seeing our superior numbers, fled at our approach. We reached Granada at 9 o'clock that morning, and entered the place playing Yankee Doodle. We continued fighting for an hour, when the enemy again left for León, General WALKER holding the town; but we were roused up every ten minutes with the alarm that the enemy were coming.

"Our next movement was when we crossed the Lake to Rivas with a portion of the troops. Here we met about 600 of the native forces; our number was about 150.

PRESIDENT WILLIAM WALKER SIGNS THE COMMISSION OF AN OFFICER IN THE NICARAGUAN ARMY IN 1857

"We fought two hours, and took their barricade; we then burnt their tents along the road; at the five-mile house we got some corn bread and some beef. The natives have muskets, with flint locks, and their machetes, (a long knife,) but we could never get near enough to them for them to use their knives. Our men had muskets with percussion locks, rifles and revolvers; and each person also had a bowie-knife in his belt. We were then recruited by two companies under Gen. WALKER, and after some further fighting a heavy rain came on. We had no tents, but each man had a blanket, and we slept on the ground; the men soon grew sick with chills, and we retreated to Masaya."

ACKER gives the narrative of the fight at Masaya in which he participated in much the same unsophisticated manner as the foregoing, confirming the main facts as given by others. He seemed disposed to put as good a face as possible upon the state of things in Nicaragua, but he evidently thinks the truth is hard enough. He had good clothing which was destroyed when Granada was burned. He became so sick as to be disabled from duty, and on three separate occasions asked General WALKER to allow him to go home, but was always refused. WALKER saying he could not pay the passage of people to "Nicaragua, and get no service out of them;"—said he, "I wish to get *service* out of you, yet."

ACKER finally availed himself of the passing of the California passengers to escape with them—the passengers kindly assisting him to get home. The general opinion prevails among the people of the Isthmus that General WALKER's position is getting desperate and that he cannot hold out much longer against the great numbers combined against him.

Although Walker's men were now in poor condition, the Central American allies had suffered even heavier losses. Their leaders were torn with dissension and unable to decide how to deliver the coup de grace to William Walker. At this point Cornelius Vanderbilt came to their aid—he wanted to get rid of the Filibuster once and for all. He sent two carefully selected agents, an American named Sylvanus Spencer and an Englishman by the name of William Webster, to Costa Rica with many cases of Minié rifles and ammunition, lots of money, and detailed plans explaining precisely how to blockade and gain control of the San Juan River—to cut off Walker's vital lifeline. Spencer, formerly an engineer on one of Vanderbilt's steamboats, had the added incentive of being a stockholder in the Accessory Transit Company, whose shares were now virtually worthless.

A Costa Rican expeditionary force of 120 men was organized

under the skillful direction of Spencer. With machetes the Costa Ricans proceeded to hack their way laboriously through a thick tropical jungle to the upper reaches of the San Carlos River, a parallel stream that flows into the San Juan River. In canoes and rafts they cautiously made their way down the San Juan River to Hipp's Point, some thirty-five miles above Greytown, where the Serapiqui River, a tributary of the San Juan, joins the main stream.

HIPP'S POINT—
MOUTH OF SERAPIQUI

A detachment of Americans was on duty to guard this strategic spot against a surprise attack by the Costa Ricans, who presumably would be coming down the Serapiqui from the south. Walker's men had carelessly neglected to post a sentry on the San Juan River side of their camp. On the evening of December 22, 1856, while the gringos were eating their dinner, they were unexpectedly attacked from the rear by the Costa Rican troops led by Spencer. The entire American garrison was killed or taken captive. The same night Spencer continued down the San Juan River to Greytown, where he seized several American river steamers.

FORT SAN CARLOS, LAKE NICARAGUA

In the meantime, some eight hundred additional Costa Rican troops under the command of General José Joaquín Mora, brother of the president, managed to reach the San Juan River to reinforce the group with Spencer. Castillo Viejo and Fort San Carlos were captured from the filibusters, as were the lake steamers *La Virgen* and *San Carlos*. General Mora took possession of Virgin Bay.

The eastern part of the Nicaraguan transit route was now totally under the control of the Costa Ricans, leaving William Walker cut off from the Atlantic. Desperately needed supplies and reinforcements were stranded at Greytown—out of reach of the beleaguered Walker on the Pacific side of Nicaragua at Rivas.

This highly successful blockade, which had commenced with

VALLEY OF SAN JUAN RIVER, NICARAGUA

the capture of Hipp's Point, was aided by the British. In January 1857, 250 fresh, well-armed recruits from New Orleans attempted to seize a steamer from Spencer and some Costa Rican soldiers near Greytown, in order to come to Walker's aid. Her Majesty's man-of-war H.M.S. *Orion* interceded in behalf of the Costa Ricans and allowed Spencer to return up the San Juan River unmolested.

Before long, three contingents of filibuster troops were detained in Greytown, unable to proceed into the interior of Nicaragua. Some of the most competent officers in the filibuster army were reluctantly hors de combat, including Colonel Frank Anderson, one of the original fifty-eight "Immortals"; General C. C. Hornsby; Charles W. Doubleday, who was later to write a book about his reminiscences of Nicaragua; and C. Roberdeau Wheat, a boyhood friend of William Walker and his brothers at the University of Nashville. A jovial, corpulent warrior, Wheat had served under Narciso López in Cuba, where he was captured and sent to a prison in Spain; later he had participated in a revolution in Mexico and acquired the rank of brigadier general in the Mexican army—a commission he gave up in order to join Walker in Nicaragua. (Subsequently Wheat was destined to lose his life in the Civil War, serving in the Confederate army as an officer with the "Louisiana Tigers.")

Despite the presence of such able combat officers, a recruiting officer named Colonel S. A. Lockridge—who had seen no active service—was designated to assume command of the filibuster troops (still technically considered recruits) in Greytown, as plans were made to recapture control of the San Juan River.

Owing largely to the heroism of Anderson, Doubleday, and Wheat, the garrison at Hipp's Point was temporarily retaken, although the Americans suffered heavy losses. Lockridge then decided that Castillo Viejo should be attacked by a company of raw, unseasoned recruits from Kansas known as "border ruffians," under the command of Colonel H. T. Titus, who was totally unfamiliar with Central American warfare. This turned out to be a disastrous strategic error.

FORT CASTILLO VIEJO, NICARAGUA

In December 1856 the Costa Ricans (aided by Cornelius Vanderbilt) gained control of the San Juan River, seized this fort, and cut off William Walker's army from much-needed supplies that had been shipped from the eastern seaboard of the United States.

Castillo Viejo was a picturesque Spanish fortress atop a steep hill at the edge of the San Juan River. When Titus and his "border ruffians" first attacked this venerable stronghold they could have taken it easily, since there were very few Costa Rican defenders. Instead of demanding immediate surrender, however, Titus foolishly allowed the Costa Ricans a reprieve of twenty-four hours so they could obtain formal permission to surrender from their commanding officer at Fort San Carlos, further up the river. By the time the period of grace had expired, so many additional Costa Rican reinforcements had arrived on the scene that Titus and his troops from Kansas had to retreat down the river in humiliating disorder.

Lockridge belatedly decided to make another attempt to capture Castillo Viejo with more experienced officers, but it was too late. The Costa Rican defenders had cleared away the undergrowth on the steep slopes of the hill below the fort, thus making it a seemingly unconquerable fortification. At least that was the opinion of the veteran filibusters Hornsby, Doubleday, and Wheat. One cannot help but wonder if William Walker himself would not have charged up the hill at Castillo Viejo anyway, in spite of the odds.

The Americans were obliged to return to Greytown; to make matters worse, on the way down the river the boiler on a river steamer exploded, killing a few filibusters and wounding many more. Hipp's Point was abandoned. Some four hundred recruits were stranded at Punta Arenas, near Greytown, under miserable conditions; many died of fever and exposure before their passage could be arranged to Panama or back to the United States. All hope of reaching Walker at Rivas was given up.

Sylvanus Spencer had carried out Vanderbilt's instructions to a T; the Costa Ricans controlled the San Juan River and Lake Nicaragua. General Mora of Costa Rica, giving little credit to Vanderbilt's money and Spencer's daring, proclaimed: "The main artery of filibusterism has been cut forever. The Costa Rican sword has severed it."

The Costa Ricans disliked Spencer and were glad to see him return to New York. He had treated the Costa Rican troops contemptuously, while he prodded them harshly to the absolute limit of their endurance.

Although General Mora belittled Spencer's efforts in the amazingly successful blockade of the San Juan River, the latter was not too disappointed. Commodore Vanderbilt in a grateful, expansive mood is said to have granted Spencer a well-earned reward of fifty thousand dollars.

California could have sent supplies to Walker, but by this time the state seems to have lost interest in the Filibuster. The South wanted to help, but the Atlantic side of Nicaragua was cut off. Walker lost all hope of aid from Morgan and Garrison: these two ineffective entrepreneurs had been forced to dock their ships and cease operations. At San Juan del Sur, British warships bottled up the harbor where the *Granada* was anchored. Walker was thus abandoned and stranded, left to his fate.

IN NEW ORLEANS, WILLIAM WALKER WAS ADMIRED AS THE "MAN OF DESTINY"

In its editorial of January 31, 1857, *Harper's Weekly* did not suspect that the downfall of the Filibuster was imminent:

> We have again and again called Walker a hero. We are obliged to recognize a persistence, an endurance, a resolute heroism which merit a higher place in human esteem than can be ceded to all the knights errant of history and Faërydom. . . . The difference is that ours is a nineteenth century hero. . . . Who knows how soon he may replace the laurel of the hero with the diadem of a king?

The diadem proved to be only a dream, about to be shattered by harsh reality. Unaware of the blockade of the San Juan River, Walker, Henningsen, and the American Phalanx consisting of about nine hundred men—supposedly the official army of the republic of Nicaragua—established themselves in Rivas in early January 1857 and prepared to withstand yet another siege, which turned out to be the last stand. Since his inauguration as president of Nicaragua some six months earlier, the Filibuster's fortunes had been going steadily downhill. Soon the bad news concerning Spencer, the events around Greytown, and the Costa Rican blockade filtered into Rivas. It must have been apparent to Walker that he had committed a fatal blunder in incurring the wrath of Cornelius Vanderbilt—if he hadn't, he might have been able to hold his own against the Central American allies who were encircling him.

In this final siege at Rivas, President Mora of Costa Rica changed his tactics. A year before he had threatened death to all captured filibusters, a warning that had only made the Americans fight harder. Mora now scattered handbills in the neighborhood of Rivas promising food, protection, and a free passage home to all who would desert Walker. This change of strategy had been recommended by Vanderbilt. What had been a war on all filibusters now became a war against only one—William Walker.

Desertions increased among Walker's troops as the supplies of chocolate, sugar, mangoes, and meat grew scarce. After all, the Americans were not fighting for their own native land. Soon the gringos even ran out of mule meat and were obliged to resort to a diet of "cats, dogs and stewed rawhide."

WALKER'S
SOLDIERS
WERE LUCKY
WHEN THEY
GOT
HARDTACK

WALKER'S STARVING AND EXHAUSTED TROOPS
RECEIVING RATIONS

In early 1857 a disenchanted deserter who had managed to escape from Rivas told his tale of woe to a correspondent of the *New-York Daily Times* in Panama:

> Many of the deserters from the "Man of Destiny" are rich in experience. It would be a profitable thing for someone of your graphic pensters to bag one of those live filibusters—take him home, wash, feed and clothe him—untangle his hair, crop his beard, scent him with *eau de rose* . . . and when he gets fat and comfortable and chatty, spread him out on the best lounge and then squeeze him. What tales of wrong, oppression, iron-heeled despotism, of hearts broken . . . innocence violated, murders, massacres, executions he would spin. Sieges, burnings and blowing-up of cities; battles on land, sea, lake and river would roll out from under his tongue, until your pen waxed weak with the record. He would tell you of God's image devoured by buzzards on the roadside; of hospitals full of cholera, fever and mortification; of tender youth, like that of the Kentucky boy, riddled with balls by the executioner for sleeping at the pickets. . . . He could gorge you with horrors. The picture would be a dark one—very dark—shaded all over—with little or nothing to relieve its sombre hue. A few moonlight serenades to the glossy-haired señoritas on the sweet balmy evenings down by the great lake, in the old city of Granada—a few flirtations with the less thoughtful and scornful of the pearly-toothed maidens of Masaya—a few fandangoes in the war-worn city of Rivas—might be thrown in. Betting away scrip—horse racing—cock-fighting—duels of chivalry—and the pleasant amusement of stripping altars of their silver, and young girls of their rings and keepsakes—might make up another chapter. Pierre Soulé's soliloquy when he laid his head upon his pillow, after negotiating with the broker in New Orleans for the sale of those little abstractions would read well. . . . But the poor deserter had got a call from his old friends, the chills and fever, by this time and must go wrap himself up in blankets, put mustard on his legs—steam himself with boiling water—take quinine, and die. The book might be dedicated to William Walker, the Man of Destiny with the blue gray eyes.

In February 1857 a United States sloop-of-war, the *St. Mary's*, arrived at the Pacific port of San Juan del Sur under the command of Commander Charles H. Davis. Davis had received instructions to protect American lives and property during the unsettled state of affairs in Nicaragua. Attempting to be neutral, he secured the permission of the belligerents to rescue women and children from the dreadful siege at Rivas and take them to the safety of San Juan del Sur, under the protection of the American flag.

SAN JUAN DEL SUR, NICARAGUA
The Transit Road passed over the gap to the right.

While this rescue was in progress, a truce was declared. The besiegers shouted to the starving, vermin-ridden filibusters, offering them plenty of food, aguardiente, and tobacco if they would give up. These assurances brought so many more desertions that Walker finally proclaimed to his remaining forces that all who wished to leave Rivas might do so. Only five men took advantage of this offer, although the end was obviously near.

General Mora advised Commander Davis that the Costa Rican troops, rather than trying to take Rivas by force, intended to starve Walker into surrendering. Davis intervened and stated that if the Americans were spared, he would force Walker to surrender to him. Walker's situation had now become desperate—he could hold out for a few days longer at most. Several messages were exchanged. Walker insisted upon protection for his native Nicaraguan allies as well as the Americans. This request was acceded to.

A document of surrender was prepared by Walker and Henningsen and delivered to Commander Davis. The surrender, dated May 1, 1857, was specifically to the United States Navy and not to the Central American allies. A total of 463 of Walker's men surrendered at Rivas. Davis's marines were to protect the troops surrendering at Rivas until transportation to the United States could be provided.

General William Walker and sixteen officers were first transported to Panama by Commander Davis and then returned to New Orleans. The remainder of Walker's army was to be conveyed to Greytown over the transit route and then taken to the United States on the U. S. frigate *Wabash*, under the command of Commodore Hiram Paulding. The Filibuster War in Nicaragua was over.

Walker's abrupt departure caused resentment among many of his disheartened followers: they felt that the "gray-eyed man of destiny" for whom they had suffered hunger, wounds, disease, fevers, and untold miseries was abandoning them in their hour of need.

Walker remained aloof. One of his final commands (against his will) was to order the reluctant and still eager Fayssoux to surrender the filibuster "navy," consisting of the little schooner *Granada*, to Commander Davis.

WORTHLESS
PAPER
CURRENCY WAS
ISSUED BY
WALKER'S
NICARAGUAN
GOVERNMENT

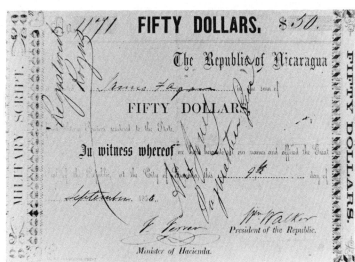

The Filibuster still trusted in destiny. He had had to surrender to Davis: he had no other choice. But looking ahead, he planned to return to Nicaragua as soon as possible to regain the heady power he had so briefly held. The agreement of surrender did not impose upon Walker any obligation *not* to return to Central America.

After the disastrous defeat at Rivas, a "normal" man might have given up; but William Walker (possibly affected by paranoia) seemed to consider himself a special agent of God, appointed to regenerate Central America.

THE ENTIRE FRONT PAGE OF THE "NEW-YORK DAILY TIMES" OF MARCH 21, 1857, WAS DEVOTED EXCLUSIVELY TO WILLIAM WALKER AND NICARAGUA

New-York Daily Times.

VOL. VI......NO. 1724.   NEW-YORK, MONDAY, MARCH 30, 1857.   PRICE TWO CENTS

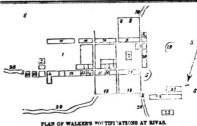

PLAN OF WALKER'S FORTIFICATIONS AT RIVAS.

1. Plaza.
2. Malabo Hacienda, used as a general hospital.

LIKEWISE, ON MARCH 30, 1857, THE FRONT PAGE NEWS OF THE "NEW-YORK DAILY TIMES" FEATURED ONLY WILLIAM WALKER AND NICARAGUA

13

Cheers at Home for the Vanquished Hero

WALKER was given a hero's welcome in New Orleans on May 27, 1857. A cheering throng met him as he was carried ashore triumphantly on the shoulders of his most ardent admirers. An hour after registering at the St. Charles Hotel he was obliged to step out on the balcony of his room and make a short speech for the benefit of the enthusiastic crowd below. The local newspapers filled their editorial columns with unbridled praise for the returning filibuster, whose projects held out hope for the preservation and extension of slavery.

A few days later Walker spoke for two hours at a mass meeting in New Orleans before twenty thousand people, standing on a platform decorated with the stars and stripes of the United States, as well as the flag of Nicaragua. He made it quite clear that he intended to return to Central America to complete the work he had started, blaming Secretary of State Marcy in Washington, Northern abolitionists, and the British government for his temporary setback. He pointed out that when he arrived in Nicaragua the political situation was in a terrible mess, even worse than it had been under the Spanish; the mongrelism of the local population rendered them incapable of self-government. He urged the Southern states to assist him in his mission of Americanizing Central America:

> I call upon you, therefore, to execute this mission . . . to regenerate
> the amalgamated race . . . to Americanize Central America. . . . I feel
> that my duty calls upon me to return [to Nicaragua]. All who are

GENERAL WILLIAM WALKER OF NICARAGUA WAS GIVEN A HERO'S WELCOME IN NEW ORLEANS AS HE ADDRESSED A LARGE CROWD FROM THE BALCONY OF THE ST. CHARLES HOTEL

nearest and dearest to me are there. There sleep the men, soldiers, and officers whose rights I cannot fail to have respected. . . . I call upon you then, fellow-citizens, male and female, whose friends and relatives have perished, to lend your aid;—upon the men to assist with their fortunes and purses; upon the mothers to belt the swords about their sons; upon the maiden as she listens to the lover at her feet, until he shall vow to go forth on the mission of his duty. Aye, fellow-citizens, I call upon you all by the glorious recollections of the past, and the bright anticipation for the future, to assist in carrying out and perfecting the Americanization of Central America.

There was tremendous applause as William Walker closed his speech. The band struck up "Yankee Doodle," and the admiring audience accompanied him en masse to the St. Charles Hotel. The reporter from the *New Orleans Sunday Times* wrote that he had never witnessed such enthusiasm among the people of New Orleans.

Wilhelmine McCord, a local belle, like many women, was carried away by Walker and wrote an impromptu poem in his honor:

> Bring music for WALKER, bring flowers for his crown,
> Let them die in his way—let his foot crush them down,
> And perfume float out on the air as they die—
> They were born for the brave, in his path let them lie.
>
> All hail to thee! Chief, Heaven's blessings may rest
> On the battle-scarred brow of our National guest,
> And soon may our Eagle fly over the sea,
> And plant there a branch of our National Tree.

Traveling northward, the Filibuster was felicitated in Memphis and joyfully welcomed in Louisville and Cincinnati. Crowds gathered at every stop to admire their hero, wondering how so much strength and determination could be packed into such a tiny body.

In early June, Walker visited President Buchanan in Washington and, stretching the truth outrageously, complained to the chief executive that if Commander Davis had not interfered, the Central American allies would have been defeated. In point of fact he owed his life to Davis, who had rescued him from the wrath of the infuriated Central Americans. A few months later Walker claimed that during this meeting Buchanan had encouraged him to make another attempt to conquer Nicaragua.

The hero worship of Walker reached its peak on June 17 in New York City. When he attended Wallack's Theatre, occupying a box with General and Mrs. Henningsen, he got a standing ovation. The cheering for the Filibuster was thunderous, as the orchestra played "Hail, Columbia." Walker was obliged to address the audience from his box and ask them to quiet down and pay attention to the play they had come to see.

Suddenly the bubble of popularity burst in the North; the press, which Walker had brusquely ignored, turned against him. The frigate *Wabash* arrived in New York harbor with 139 wretched, desperate refugees from Walker's army in Nicaragua, leftovers from the siege at Rivas, including 13 women and 5 children. Prolonged suffering and starvation had reduced most of these sick and destitute people to pitiable skeletons dressed in rags. The men were so covered with lice that they had infested the ship, forcing the officers of the *Wabash* to bathe in rum. The reporters who boarded the ship found nothing but misery and bitter criticism of William Walker, who was accused of despicable cowardice for deserting his beleaguered troops in their hour of need. This revelation made good copy for the New York press, which proceeded to denounce the Filibuster harshly, criticizing him for cruelty, lack of compassion, cold cynicism, and various other shortcomings.

Instead of replying to these accusations and visiting his distressed comrades, Walker abruptly left town.

HARPER'S WEEKLY.

SATURDAY, JUNE 6, 1857.

WHAT IS TO BECOME OF NICARAGUA?

WE this week communicate to our readers a startling piece of intelligence—nothing less than the flight of General William Walker, with the remainder of his men, from Nicaragua, and their safe arrival in the United States. At New Orleans, we are told, Walker was received with enthusiasm by the people; here the press concurs in pronouncing a verdict of "served him right." Of the two, our people are nearest common sense.

When a man undertakes to make war, either for his own advancement or from motives of public policy, he has no choice but to succeed or to be doomed to execration. History may do justice to the unfortunate adventurer, but the world prudently judges enterprises by their issue, and interprets failure as the equivalent of unwholesome intention. There is—and perhaps it is well—no pity for the conquered.

Let William Walker, then, be visited with the hatred and contempt which are the meed of the conquered. Let his name be a warning to all enterprising youths to respect the territory of their neighbors, and on no account to attempt to spread civilization and commerce by processes ignored by the neutrality laws. Let him be set on a pinnacle of scorn and ignominy to be hooted and scouted by intelligent millions of human beings.

NO PITY
FOR THE
CONQUERED

14

The Second Effort

WALKER seemed immune both to praise and criticism.
Ignoring the caustic comments of the New York newspapers,
which claimed he had "sneaked away," he had, in fact, departed
for Charleston, Nashville, and Mobile with the object of forming the secret Central American League, with branches in the
principal cities of the United States. This clandestine organization was set up in order to finance a second filibustering expedition to Nicaragua, on a much larger scale than the first.

Although the government in Washington was hostile to filibustering, a large section of the public still favored and supported it—especially in the South.

The financial depression of 1857 made it difficult to raise
money. Recruiting was no problem: many young Southerners
were eager to fight with Walker. Eventually enough funds were
collected to enable one of the Filibuster's secret agents to buy
a steamship in New Orleans called the *Fashion*, as well as a
substantial quantity of arms and military supplies. Although
blocked by federal marshals in New Orleans, the Filibuster,
with 270 men (including 6 of the original Immortals) managed
to put to sea from Mobile Bay on November 14, 1857.

President Buchanan was irritated that Walker had flaunted
U. S. neutrality laws and instructed his secretary of the navy
to intercept the *Fashion*. The sloop-of-war *Saratoga* was ordered to the Nicaraguan harbor of Greytown.

SAN JUAN DEL NORTE (GREYTOWN)

This Caribbean seaport on the eastern coast of Nicaragua was called Greytown during many years of British influence. At the mouth of the San Juan River, it was for centuries the entrance to the most feasible route across Nicaragua. During the 1890s a canal was started here, then abandoned.

Meanwhile, when the *Fashion* neared Nicaragua after nine days at sea, it headed for the mouth of the Colorado River, a fork of the San Juan several miles south of Greytown. Three boats were lowered, and a company of recruits under the command of the veteran Frank Anderson were ordered by Walker to surprise the Costa Ricans holding the Accessory Transit Company steamers on the San Juan River and then capture Fort Castillo Viejo, midway up the river.

The *Fashion* put out to sea again and quietly approached Greytown, where the *Saratoga,* under Commander Frederick Chatard, was waiting to prevent the filibusters from landing.

Suddenly two hundred armed men were ashore and making camp before the chagrined commander of the *Saratoga* realized what was happening. Walker and his remaining troops waited anxiously in the rain for several days, on a dreary, sandy camping ground, hoping for good news from Anderson.

Anderson was highly successful in his mission. Within a few days he had captured three river steamers, a lake steamer, and Fort Castillo Viejo from the Costa Ricans without losing a man. When this favorable information reached Walker's camp it caused boundless joy—which, however, was destined to be short-lived. The following morning the *Saratoga* was joined by the fifty-gun steam frigate *Wabash*, commanded by Commodore Hiram Paulding, U. S. N.; the next day the U. S. man-of-war *Fulton*, as well as two British war vessels, dropped anchor nearby—all intent upon checking and frustrating William Walker and his filibusters.

Several small boats from the *Saratoga* were sent up the San Juan River to form a blockade to prevent Walker's men from ascending it. Commodore Paulding informed Walker that he and all his men were to surrender at once, to become prisoners of the United States. This was no idle threat: the *Saratoga* moved in toward shore and trained her guns broadside, at point-blank range, at the filibusters' camp.

Walker's position was utterly hopeless. His second invasion of Nicaragua, off to such a promising start thanks to Anderson's river victories, was now doomed to abortive failure. Having no alternative and wishing to avoid needless bloodshed, Walker complied with the orders of Commodore Paulding and surrendered once again to United States authorities.

Paulding, a large, robust, ambitious officer, summoned Walker to his quarters and proceeded to scold the shabby little filibuster: "You and your men are a disgrace to the United States. You have dishonored your country. You are no better than pirates and murderers." For once Walker was at a loss for words as his self-control cracked, strained beyond its limits by frustration, rage, and another humiliating fiasco. Paulding described their emotional confrontation in a letter to his wife:

HIRAM PAULDING, COMMODORE, U.S.N.

This lion-hearted devil, who had so often destroyed the lives of other men, came to me, humbled himself, and wept like a child. . . . I have had him in the cabin since as my guest. We laugh and talk as though nothing had happened, and you would think, to see him with the captain and myself, that he was one of us. He is a sharp fellow and requires a sharp fellow to deal with him.

Most of the filibusters were placed aboard the *Saratoga* and on December 12, 1857, less than a month after their departure from Mobile, were forced to return to the United States. Walker was taken to Panama, and then transported to New York on parole to offer himself for arrest to the United States marshal. The Filibuster proceeded immediately to Washington

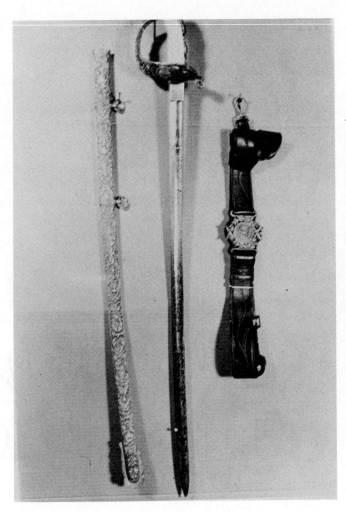

THE REPUBLIC OF NICARAGUA PRESENTED THIS SABER AND SCABBARD TO COMMODORE HIRAM PAULDING, UNITED STATES NAVY, IN RECOGNITION OF HIS CAPTURE OF THE FILIBUSTER WILLIAM WALKER ON DECEMBER 8, 1857, DURING WALKER'S SECOND ATTEMPT TO INVADE NICARAGUA

to protest vigorously Paulding's action at Greytown: an American officer had invaded the territory of a friendly power and insulted its flag by arresting the filibusters on Nicaraguan soil.

Indignant meetings were held in the South, condemning Paulding and praising Walker. Some even demanded that Walker and his men be returned to Nicaragua on a United States vessel. President Buchanan seemed to be ambivalent about this controversy: he criticized Paulding for being over-zealous, and Walker for violating United States neutrality laws.

The Walker-Paulding case was aired in both houses of Congress in January 1858. For several days the subject was debated fervently, and all other business was set aside while Walker and Paulding were either severely denounced or ardently defended. Finally the exhausted Congress and the president reached a compromise: all resolutions were dropped and Paulding was mildly censured and temporarily relieved of his command. At the same time, it was quite apparent that President Buchanan had repudiated filibusterism and was against the idea of annexing any part of Central America to the United States.

WILLIAM WALKER IS REMEMBERED IN NEW ORLEANS
This trial took place in June 1858 when Southern juries were ardently pro-Walker.

Washington Jan. 5th 1858

Colonel:

I received your report yesterday. It is satisfactory and valuable.

Capt. Fayssoux will receive a letter from me at the same time you get this. Co-operate with him according to the instructions of my letter.

In a short time we will all be back in Nicaragua.

Your obdt servt

Wm Walker

Col. B. Natzmer.

IN 1858 WALKER WAS PLANNING TO RETURN TO NICARAGUA TO TRY TO REGAIN HIS LOST POWER, AS NOTED IN THIS LETTER TO A FORMER AIDE, COLONEL BRUNO VON NATZMER

In June 1858 William Walker and Frank Anderson were brought to trial in New Orleans for violation of the Neutrality Law of 1818, in connection with their unsuccessful filibustering expedition to Nicaragua of November–December 1857. Pierre Soulé and Walker himself defended them. Ten of the jurors voted for acquittal and two for conviction. Walker, having nothing to fear from Southern judges and juries, demanded another trial in hopes of gaining total acquittal. The district attorney entered a nolle prosequi on the record, however, and the case was dropped.

William Walker, after two failures in Nicaragua, was a fallen idol in the North but still highly regarded in the South. He started on a lengthy, successful lecture tour of Southern cities to raise money for a third expedition to Nicaragua. He was received with genuine enthusiasm and received many honors. In Alabama a charter was granted to the Mobile and Nicaragua

MOBILE, OCTOBER 4, 1858.

SIR:—

You are advised that on the 10th day of November next, a Vessel will leave this Port for SAN JUAN-DEL NORTE. She will take any Passengers and Freight that may offer for NICARAGUA.

If you, or any persons in your neighborhood, desire to EMIGRATE to CENTRAL AMERICA, please advise me of it as soon as possible, in order that passages may be secured for you and your companions.

It will be well for you to arrive here three or four days previous to the day of departure.

Your Obedient Servant,

Wm. Walker

IN OCTOBER 1858 WILLIAM WALKER ATTEMPTED A COMEBACK: SOME 150 RECRUITS LEFT FOR NICARAGUA BUT WHEN THEIR SHIP RAN AGROUND IN BRITISH HONDURAS, THE EXPEDITION FAILED

Steamship Company organized by Southern sympathizers to support Walker. The Central American League was revived under a new title: the Southern Emigration Society.

Walker soon determined to send another group of about 150 "colonizers" from Mobile to Central America on the sailing vessel *Susan*, under the command of two veteran filibusters, Frank Anderson and C. W. Doubleday. Walker himself planned to follow them in another ship. This was destined to be a very short and ignominious filibustering expedition: the *Susan* went aground on a coral reef near British Honduras on December 16, 1858, and the recruits were rescued by a British warship and brought back to Mobile.

The stricter neutrality laws enforced a period of relative leisure upon William Walker. During 1859 and early 1860, having been offered a contract by the publishers S. H. Goetzel of Mobile to write a book about his experiences in Nicaragua, Walker made use of his facile journalistic talent and wrote *The War in Nicaragua*. Written in fluent disciplined prose, the book dispassionately described the magnificent landscape of Nicaragua, exposed the shoddy politics of Central America,

Phil⁰ March 30ᵗʰ 1859

My dear Sir

The news by the Steamer from Aspinwall that Genᵗ Wm Walker had arrived at that place under an assumed name is incorrect. Mr Walker left Mobile with the intention of going to California via New Orleans. When he arrived in N.O. he received letters of such an encouraging character and had so many assurances from his friends there, that he changed his mind, and still remains in N.O. with a view of perfecting his intentions of "managing emigration to Nicaragua". His own opinion is that his prospects are now brighter than ever. He is more busy

than ever in his preparations. You can rely upon this information. He is encouraged by those interests in Central America opposed to Martinez.

very respectfully
Your friend as ever
James C. Van Dyke

To the President.

AN INTELLIGENCE REPORT

In March 1859 James C. Van Dyke, a confidant of James Buchanan, informed the president that William Walker, encouraged by friends in New Orleans, was preparing another invasion of Nicaragua.

JAMES BUCHANAN, PRESIDENT OF THE UNITED STATES
(1857–61)

At first Buchanan supported William Walker, but as the Civil War grew nearer gradually turned against him. Buchanan was from Pennsylvania, while Walker was a hero of the slave states of the South.

and gave an accurate firsthand account of the filibusters' military campaigns in Nicaragua, including victories and defeats. Walker expressed his regrets for valiant comrades lost and his contempt for North American politicians. Then, leaving truthfulness to one side, he indulged himself in some far-fetched racist, proslavery propaganda, as he exhorted the South to introduce African slavery to Nicaragua immediately:

> If we look at Africa in the light of universal history, we see her for more than five thousand years a mere waif on the waters of the world, fulfilling no part in its destinies, and aiding in no manner the progress of general civilization. Sunk in the depravities of fetichism, and reeking with the blood of human sacrifices, she seemed a satire on man, fit only to provoke the sneer of devils at the wisdom, and justice, and benevolence of the Creator. But America was discovered, and the European found the African a useful auxiliary in subduing the new continent to the uses and purposes of civilization. . . . The labor of the inferior races cannot compete with that of the white race unless you give it a white master to direct its energies; and without such protection as slavery affords, the colored races must inevitably succumb in the struggle with white labor. . . . In Nicaragua the negro seems to be in his natural climate. The blacks who have gone thither from Jamaica are healthy, strong and capable of severe labor. . . . In fact, the negro blood seems to assert its superiority over the indigenous Indian of Nicaragua. . . . Time presses. If the South wishes to get her institutions into tropical America she must do so before treaties are made to embarrass her action and hamper her energies . . . in the effort to re-establish slavery in Central America. . . . The hearts of Southern youth answer to the call of honor, and strong arms and steady eyes are waiting to carry forward the policy which is now the dictate of duty as well as of interest. . . . Something is due from the South to the memory of the brave dead who repose in the soil of Nicaragua. . . . The true field for the exertion of slavery is in tropical America.

In *The War in Nicaragua* Walker produced a curious blend of precise fact and bigoted prejudice, always referring to himself in the third person. Perhaps he realized, at the age of thirty-five, that he was a failure fanatically struggling for a lost cause, that he had indeed been defeated. But he could not bring himself to make such admissions, even in the third person. Perhaps as he wrote certain calamitous incidents came back to disturb him, such as the death sentences he had imposed on Mateo Mayorga, Ponciano Corral, and countless others.

GENERAL WILLIAM WALKER
"A piercing eye, a princely air,
A presence like a chevalier,
Half angel and half Lucifer."
(From "With Walker in Nicaragua," by Joaquin Miller)

For whatever reason, he gradually turned to religion—not the strict Tennessee Protestantism of his father but to Roman Catholicism. He became a Catholic. This conversion may have been another step toward a return to Central America, where he felt some prejudice had existed against him because he was a Protestant; or perhaps it was prompted by a vague foreboding of ominous events soon to take place.

Meanwhile, a venturesome clandestine organization was growing in importance in the South. The Knights of the Golden Circle, a jingoist fraternal order with strong, proslavery aims was formed, reaching the zenith of its short-lived fame in 1859–60. The phrase Golden Circle in its title came from its basic design: Havana was to be the center of a giant circle with a radius of approximately twelve hundred miles, which would include Maryland, Kentucky, all the Southern states, most of Texas and Mexico, all of Central America, all of the West Indies, and the northern tip of South America. This fertile region, rich in cotton, tobacco, sugar, rice, and coffee, would become a huge slave empire, ruled by Anglo-Saxons, that would rival the Roman Empire in prestige and power—a dazzling dream for disgruntled slaveholders. The South was informed that, if the Knights of the Golden Circle were successful, twenty-five additional slave states, carved from this vast new territory, would be added to the American Union, along with fifty more Southern senators.

The inspirational organizer and permanent president of the K. G. C. was a Virginian, George W. L. Bickley—known to his followers as "the General"—who, like William Walker, had been a physician and journalist before becoming an adventurer.

Although Bickley never got around to carrying out his pet scheme, which in 1859 was the military invasion and "Texasing" of Mexico, he was for a time a notorious and fanatical armchair filibuster with a facile pen—an enthusiastic promoter of the southward march of Manifest Destiny, who envisioned himself as the future emperor of Mexico.

Bickley's K. G. C. was an elaborate fraternal and secret organization—so secret in fact that it is not known to this day how many thousands of Southern Knights joined its ranks (Bickley claimed sixty-five thousand, although the true figure in all probability was much smaller). The zealous Knights were grouped into categories such as Foreign Guards, Home Guard, American Legion, Volunteer Auxiliaries, and so on, of first, second, and third degree. The regional lodges were known as "castles." This top-secret fraternal organization was provided by General Bickley with an intricate set of rituals, codes, signs, and mysterious passwords known only to the initiated. Admission payments, fees, and dues were of course required of members. Some enemies of Bickley suggested that he was a charlatan, a coward, and a get-rich-quick promoter. Bickley, following Walker's example in Nicaragua, promised his cohorts (many of whom were Texans) substantial pay and generous grants of 640 acres of Mexican land, provided the invasion of Mexico—which never took place—succeeded. Like Walker in Nicaragua, Bickley claimed he would regenerate the polyglot, hybrid population of Spanish America.

Unlike Walker, however, Bickley never got around to leading his mysterious troops into bloody battle. It is said Walker's misfortunes in Central America may have discouraged the more cautious Bickley and caused him to delay indefinitely his own quixotic invasion of Mexico.

After the outbreak of the Civil War, Bickley served for a time as a surgeon in the Confederate army until he was captured and imprisoned by Northern authorities. Upon his death in 1867 he faded into oblivion, along with his fanatical Knights of the Golden Circle.

15

Attempted Invasion of Honduras

WALKER went to Louisville in April 1860 to visit his sister, Mrs. Alice Richardson. It was the last quiet springtime before the Civil War—and also Walker's last springtime. Upon his return to New Orleans he received some exciting news: an Englishman had come to New Orleans on behalf of the British community on the Caribbean island of Ruatan, in the Bay of Honduras. In July 1860 England was planning to turn Ruatan over to Honduras in exchange for commercial concessions on the mainland of that republic (Her Majesty's government had become more conciliatory toward Central America following Walker's defeat three years earlier). Most Englishmen on the island were against this project and planned to defy Honduras when the time came, then set up an independent government. Would William Walker help them in a war with Honduras?

The prospect for military action appealed to Walker. Although he was a fallen star, headed for somber oblivion, he would not give up. He proceeded to formulate another grand plan of which Ruatan would be only the starting point: with the help of the ex-president of Honduras, Trinidad Cabañas, currently out of office and trying to regain the presidency, Honduras would be conquered; then with the help of a mighty filibuster army, Nicaragua and Costa Rica would be defeated. A Central American slave federation would eventually be established with William Walker as the "regenerator" and dictator.

196

A preliminary trip to Ruatan was made by Walker (under the pseudonym of Williams) to study the territory and plan the revolt. The picturesque uninhabited island of Cozumel (today a Mexican tourist resort) was to be used as a secret meeting place and supply depot.

Returning to the United States, Walker organized the main body of a new filibustering expedition of about one hundred men, which sailed from Mobile in June 1860 on the schooner *J. E. Taylor*. Another schooner, the *Clifton*, loaded with military supplies, sailed from New Orleans and was supposed to meet Walker near Ruatan. The British authorities, however, got wind of Walker's plans and seized the cargo of the *Clifton* at Belize. The government of Honduras, following Great Britain's suggestion, readily agreed to postpone taking possession of Ruatan in order to thwart Walker's planned invasion of the island.

Walker's filibustering forces were now obliged to wait at Cozumel for three weeks, during heavy rains, for supplies from New Orleans that never were to arrive and for the British flag to be lowered at Ruatan, an event that also did not take place.

Realizing belatedly that it would be impossible to attack Ruatan with a British warship in its harbor and with British soldiers guarding the island, Walker decided to resort to the desperate plan of attacking the old stone fortress that guarded the port of Truxillo, on the mainland of Honduras. Perhaps once Truxillo was taken, all of Honduras could be conquered with the assistance of Cabañas. The Filibuster discussed this risky project with his men, who supported him 100 percent.

Sailing in darkness, Walker hoped to surprise the garrison at Truxillo. But some fishermen saw the Americans, and the Honduran defenders were alerted.

During the night of August 5, 1860, some ninety-one Americans landed on the bay shore about two miles from the town of Truxillo. Walker and Colonel Thomas Henry led the column of filibusters silently along the beach toward the ancient Spanish fortress that protected the town. By the early light of dawn on August 6, the Hondurans commenced firing sporad-

GENERAL WALKER.—FROM A PHOTOGRAPH BY MEADE (BROTHERS), NEW YORK.

by the cowardice of some, the incapacity of others, and the treachery of many, the army has yet written a page of American history which it is impossible to forget or erase. From the future, if not from the present, we may expect just judgment.

At New Orleans, and at other large towns in the Southern States, Gen. Walker has been received with great honours; and his friends confidently assert that he will go back to Nicaragua in less than sixty days, with abundance of men and means.

A salute of 100 guns announced to the people of San José the surrender of the Filibusters. The ringing of bells, music, and cries of rejoicing manifested the enthusiasm of the people for the victors and for the re-establishment of peace. The towns and villages were illuminated during the night. Everywhere there were music, fireworks, promenades, balls, and merry réunions, and the national flag waving over all houses.

The President of the Costa Rican Republic subsequently issued a proclamation, in which he states:—

Fellow-countrymen,—The war is ended. Beloved peace comes back to us with the conquerors of Filibusterism. We have long striven, with union and constancy, for the most holy rights. God has given us the victory. There are no longer Filibusters in Central America. The few hundred of them that exist, unarmed and surrendered, are under the sanctity of our protection and clemency.

The following abridgment of the statistics of Walker's campaign in Central America (which may be divided into three periods) is taken from a detailed account by Gen. Henningsen, Walker's comrade in arms:—

The first period may be computed from the 29th January, 1855, to the 11th of April, 1856, comprising nine months, during which time Walker fought against 4800 men; viz., 1800 serviles, 3000 Costa Ricans. The result left him master of the whole territory of Nicaragua, after a loss to the enemy in round numbers of 1600 killed and wounded, and 200 to his own forces.

The second period may be reckoned from 1st September, 1856, to December 12th of the same year, terminating with the siege of Granada. During this time he had to contend against about 7000 men of the native and allied forces, the result being a loss of 311 killed and wounded on his part, and that of

over 2700 killed and wound
At the end of December th
to 1600 men, who were be
desertion. In fact, but for
river steamers, through E
might have been considered

The third period may be
January, 1857, to the 1st
minated the siege of Riva
Walker had contended aga
with a loss to his force of 3
between 2500 and 2800 to th

The force of Walker, from
Nicaragua to the 1st of M
two years—exclusive of L
The total force of the allie
Ricans said to have been on
this number 11,500 men we
Rica, Honduras, and Salva
wounded of Walker's force
of allies killed and wounde

This is without counting
died of disease. The morta
was very great. Two Ger
Granada; and in April, 185
from Rivas with Mora, at
only 500 entering San José

To this force of 2518—th
under arms during two yea
country—it is hardly nec
citizens who fought at Gran
were, with a score of exce
and it must be borne in min
died, a large proportion of

It is estimated that, dur
listed or holding commissi
or died of wounds or sickn
discharged, 430 were at Riv
80 in garrison or on steamer
—leaving 53 unaccounted fo

It will be perceived that
contest, either as regards
Walker's men fought, or th
were pitted; and to enable
this has been no holiday we
out that, in proportion to th
of the Americans in this w
more than double the num
Mexico by Taylor or Scott, a
engaged against an average
disparity of force which the
to struggle against in Mexic

OF ST. JUAN.

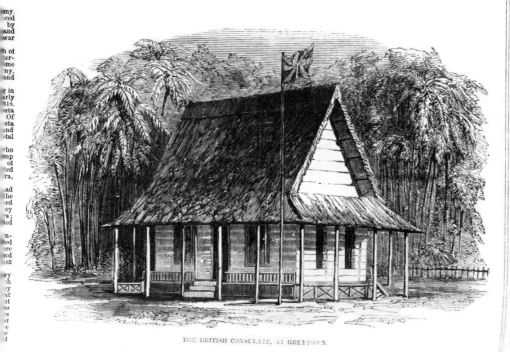

THE BRITISH CONSULATE, AT GREYTOWN.

WILLIAM WALKER WAS NOT FAMOUS ONLY IN UNITED STATES
NEWSPAPERS: THE "ILLUSTRATED LONDON NEWS" COVERED HIS
ACTIVITIES IN 1857

ically as the Americans came into view. Colonel Henry asked for volunteers to expose themselves and draw as much fire as possible from the guns of the fort. When six men promptly stepped forward, the Hondurans rapidly started shooting at them. Meanwhile the rest of the American force, after a strategic pause, rushed forward to the base of the formidable eight-foot stone walls of the fortress. Without a moment's hesitation, urged upward and onward by Colonel Henry's hoarse cheers, several Americans mounted the shoulders of their companions and climbed over the walls before the defenders could reload their muskets. Once over the top, the attacking gringos fired their revolvers furiously, right and left, with reckless abandon.

Unprepared for such terrifying heroics, those Honduran defenders who were not killed immediately took to their heels like frightened sheep and ran out of the fort. Six Americans were killed and several others wounded in this daring assault as the fortress and town of Truxillo were captured. The flag of Honduras was lowered; in its place Walker raised the colors of his dreaded filibuster flag.

The filibusters proceeded to establish themselves in the fort, overhauled and remantled many guns, and prepared for a long stay. Walker abolished customs duties and declared Truxillo a free port; he hoped to damage the economy of the government of Honduras by cutting off the Truxillo duties. This act turned out to be a serious blunder, since all customs revenues from Truxillo were supposed to be turned over to the British government to pay off an old debt. Some three thousand dollars reserved for the British tax collector disappeared in a mysterious way that no one could explain.

A correspondent for the *New York Herald* who had been with Walker at Cozumel now reported upon this attack: "THE WALKER EXPEDITION—SUDDEN DESCENT ON HONDURAS—CAPTURE OF TRUXILLO," read the headline. The heroic exploits of William Walker made good copy for other newspapers too, especially in the South. It was reported that Walker was on his way to the conquest of Central America—again.

But the Filibuster himself realized that his situation was

THE SAME JAMES CARSON JAMISON
FIFTY YEARS LATER
In 1909 he wrote a book "With Walker in Nicaragua," giving his reminiscences as an officer of the American Phalanx in Nicaragua in 1855–57.

JAMES CARSON JAMISON IN 1857
After his return from Nicaragua, where he had been an infantry captain in William Walker's army.

desperate: he needed supplies immediately or he would be starved out. There were rumors that Trinidad Cabañas, a rebel Honduran Liberal who had been exiled from his native land by President Santos Guardiola, was not far away. Grasping at a straw, Walker sent a fearless, experienced campaigner, Colonel Thomas Henry, to go out and look for Cabañas. It was a fruitless search. Henry, a veteran of the Mexican War and many Nicaraguan battles, limped back a few days later in a bad humor. Before he reported back to Walker he got drunk and got into a fight with a young filibuster lieutenant, who shot him; the bullet shattered Henry's jawbone and tore away the lower part of his face. Henry was well known for his violent temper and was constantly involved in arguments, scuffles, and duels, having been wounded many times. In the Mexican War he had distinguished himself by being one of the first to scale the walls of Chapultepec even though he was seriously injured at the time. When not fighting the enemy he relished engaging in private duels with his companions in arms; in one such altercation in Nicaragua his thighbone had been broken, which lamed him for life. A comrade said of Henry: "He could no more refrain from a duel than a boy could keep away from a game of marbles."

For two weeks the wounded man lingered, unable to talk. Walker stayed at his bedside. The speechless hulk, in great agony, could provide little information for the Filibuster. Finally a slate was put in Henry's hands in the hope that he could scrawl something coherent concerning the whereabouts of Cabañas before the spreading gangrene worsened—maggots had already eaten away most of his face. But it was no use. Walker left a full bottle of morphine at Henry's side, gave his shoulder a farewell squeeze, and walked away. The moribund veteran forced himself into an upright position, dumped the drug into a tin cup that contained lemonade, stirred the mixture, and poured it down his throat. Then he turned his face to the wall, pulled a blanket over himself, and went to sleep, never to wake again.

Meanwhile, the British warship *Icarus* had arrived at Truxillo, under the command of Captain Norvell Salmon. Salmon sent Walker a note demanding that he lay down his arms, return the money that had been illegally taken from the customhouse, and reembark, leaving his military supplies behind him. If Walker complied with these demands, the British flag would guarantee the safety and personal property of the filibusters.

In order to gain time, Walker replied that he knew nothing about the money and asked Salmon for further details of the proposed surrender. Additional notes were exchanged. Under cover of darkness Walker and some sixty-five men made a quiet but hasty departure from the fort and marched eastward along the coast to look for Cabañas.

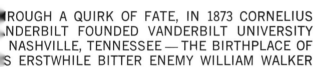

ROUGH A QUIRK OF FATE, IN 1873 CORNELIUS
NDERBILT FOUNDED VANDERBILT UNIVERSITY
NASHVILLE, TENNESSEE — THE BIRTHPLACE OF
S ERSTWHILE BITTER ENEMY WILLIAM WALKER

A native guide who said he knew where Cabañas could be
found led the filibusters. By this time the town of Truxillo had
been surrounded by Honduran infantry, and Walker's men were
soon observed and followed. At sunrise, when the group
stopped to rest and eat a scanty breakfast beside a stream, the
Hondurans opened fire at short range, wounding some twenty
filibusters, including Walker, and killing one man. Walker,
although struck on the cheek by a musket shot, called upon his
men to return the enemy fire and beat off the attack. For
several days the Filibuster and his men struggled along the
shore, sometimes in the thorny underbrush, sometimes on the
beach, constantly harassed by the nagging sniping of the pur-
suing Honduran soldiers. Following further losses they finally
reached the Río Negro, only to find an abandoned military
camp—no Cabañas. By now there were thirty-one filibusters

left, most of them wounded. Walker, himself wounded and sick with fever, decided to dig in and fight it out, for the position was well defended with a line of abandoned rifle pits. Day and night the Hondurans kept on firing.

On September 3 Captain Salmon took two boats and forty men up the Río Negro to look for Walker. When Walker's men were sighted, the British cheered and ran up the Union Jack. Walker ordered his men to cease firing, and Captain Salmon and the Filibuster conferred. When Salmon demanded immediate surrender, Walker asked whether the demand was made by a British officer and if the surrender would be to British authority. Salmon replied: "Yes, you surrender to me as a British officer." After a few minutes' deliberation, Walker ordered his men to lay down their arms and surrender to Her Majesty's government. The exhausted filibusters were relieved to fall into the hands of British, instead of Honduran, soldiers. As he gave up his sword and pistol, Walker was again assured by Salmon that the filibusters were surrendering "to Her Britannic Majesty."

Within a few hours the British boats had transported Walker and his surviving troops to the *Icarus,* Walker being the last to go aboard. When asked who he was, he replied: "I am William Walker, president of Nicaragua." Colonel A. F. Rudler, General Walker's chief of staff, had answered at first that he was an American, but now he stepped forward to say he was a Nicaraguan and to share Walker's fate.

16

Walker's Execution at Truxillo

CAPTAIN SALMON ordered the *Icarus* to proceed at full steam to Truxillo. He announced that Walker and Rudler were to be handed over to the Honduran authorities, while the others, as Americans, were to be held as prisoners, protected by the British flag.

Walker was surprised and indignant. When they reached Truxillo, he dictated a short memorandum of protest to the correspondent of the *New York Herald*:

On board the Steamer *Icarus*
Sept. 5, 1860.

I hereby protest before the civilized world that when I surrendered to the captain of Her Majesty's steamer *Icarus*, that officer expressly received my sword and pistol, as well as the arms of Colonel Rudler, and the surrender was expressly made in so many words to him, as the representative of Her Britannic Majesty.

William Walker

At Truxillo some Honduran soldiers shoved Walker into an improvised cell in the very fort that he had abandoned six weeks earlier. He spent the last six days of his life in meditation and prayer—that is how long it took for the courier to return from Tegucigalpa with approval of the Filibuster's death sentence by his erstwhile foe, Santos Guardiola, the "butcher of Honduras," now president of the country. Rudler was sentenced to four years' imprisonment (he was subsequently pardoned). Walker's sixty-eight remaining men were permitted to return to the United States.

In his cell, shackled in heavy irons, the Filibuster was quiet and courteous. He asked to see a Catholic priest. He wanted to make sure that his soldiers were not going to be punished and was relieved to hear that Colonel Rudler would not be executed. He confessed to the priest that his political career was finished and that he was prepared to die.

At eight o'clock on the morning of September 12, 1860, a detachment of barefoot soldiers led William Walker, carrying a crucifix in one hand and flanked by two priests, to the place of execution—a ruined wall about a quarter of a mile outside Truxillo. His bearing was calm as he gave his undivided attention to the murmured consolations of the priests, ignoring the derisive jeers and taunts of a jubilant Honduran crowd that had gathered.

The procession halted near an old garrison building; the priests administered the last rites to Walker and withdrew. The Filibuster stood erect, facing impassively the ragged soldiers who were about to execute him. First one squad fired,

WALKER'S LAST LETTER — TWO DAYS BEFORE HIS EXECUTION

then a second, and as the body fell to the ground, quivering in the agony of death, an officer stepped forward to administer the coup de grace to the head, mutilating it horribly. The crowd cheered as the troops marched back to town at a lively step, leaving Walker's lifeless form stretched out in the dust.

The United States consul in Truxillo paid ten Honduran pesos for a roughhewn coffin. William Walker's interment in a cemetery outside Truxillo was routine, conducted in accordance with the rites of the Catholic Church. (Later an effort was made to bring the Filibuster's remains back to Nashville for burial, but the Honduran authorities refused permission.) The Honduran government presented Walker's sword to the government of Nicaragua.

Captain Salmon was subjected to severe criticism in United States newspapers for his fatal deception of Walker and for handing him over to the Hondurans for certain execution, after promising him the protection of the British flag. This deceitful action by Salmon did not seem to be in keeping with the very high sense of honor among officers of the British navy. Her Majesty's government, however, looked the other way, and this incident did not interfere with Salmon's subsequent naval career. The fact is that both Great Britain and the Central American republics were glad to be rid of William Walker once and for all. So was President Buchanan, who chose to forget that he had been elected in 1856 on a Democratic platform one plank of which called for the support of William Walker in Nicaragua. In his message to the Congress in December 1860, Buchanan stated:

> I congratulate you on the public sentiment which now exists, against the crime of setting on foot military expeditions within the limits of the United States, to proceed from thence and make war upon the people of unoffending states with whom we are at peace. In this respect a happy change has been effected since the commencement of my administration.

THE EXECUTION OF WILLIAM WALKER IN TRUXILLO, HONDURAS,
SEPTEMBER 12, 1860

WALKER'S GRAVE IN
TRUXILLO, HONDURAS

17

Afterthoughts

WALKER was dead—the last as well as the greatest of American filibusters. His dream of "regenerating" Central America had vanished. Filibustering activity was interrupted by the Civil War and never again became the problem it had been during the 1850s. The impetus of Manifest Destiny slowed down as the increasing industrialization of the United States checked the hunger to acquire more territory. The abolition of slavery probably gave filibustering its death blow.

Between 1850 and 1860 filibusters were constantly in trouble in United States courts, although public sentiment favored them. When President Buchanan placed United States naval vessels in Central American ports to check filibustering in 1857, it was the beginning of the end. Perhaps William Walker would have succeeded if he had been given stronger support by the United States government. As it was, he failed, bringing sorrow and misery to all concerned and drenching Nicaragua in blood. His filibustering efforts caused enormous destruction of life and property; in Central America, especially in Nicaragua and Costa Rica, a suspicion was created toward North Americans, gringos, that continues up to the present day. In an attractive brochure prepared recently by the Costa Rican Institute of Tourism, for example, not only are the natural beauty, climate, flora, fauna, economy, sports, clubs, education, hotels, and other points of interest described, but in the section on the history of Costa Rica, the Filibuster is remembered:

210

War was later [1856] waged against William Walker, an adventurer from the United States who had made himself dictator of Nicaragua, and in whose defeat, President Juan Rafael Mora played a prominent role that elevated him into a national hero.

In the last century, however, there were many loyal apologists for William Walker (mostly ardent proslavery enthusiasts), who claimed that if he had lived and succeeded in his aims he would have changed the political history of the Central American republics for the better, and saved Central America from being a constant hotbed of ever-recurring revolutions and a turbulent region beset by poverty and social disorder.

The Central Americans themselves were, for the most part, violently opposed to William Walker. In a negative way he exerted a beneficial influence on them: once they became aware of the danger he presented, the Central American republics became united to a degree that they had never been before and have never been since. Shortly after the Filibuster arrived in Nicaragua, the *Gaceta de Guatemala,* in an editorial dated November 23, 1855, had had this to say:

In Granada, Nicaragua, a newspaper is being published called El Nicaraguense—two-thirds in English. Grandiose promises are made concerning the future of Nicaragua and all of Central America due to William Walker's exploits: the resources of Nicaragua are to be developed to such an extent that great cities such as Philadelphia, New York, etc. will be built where today only the miserable towns of León, Granada and Realejo exist.

The *Gaceta de Guatemala* warned Nicaraguans to *look out* and *beware:* otherwise they would soon lose their language, religion, social customs, and Spanish-American traditions. They would be humiliated, scorned, and driven into a miserable corner of Nicaragua, prisoners of foreign exploiters.

It is virtually impossible today to arrive at an exact figure for the number of "foreign exploiters" who served under William Walker in Nicaragua during 1855–57. General Henningsen estimated that there were approximately twenty-six hundred, with no more than eight hundred taking part in any one engagement. On the other hand, Joseph N. Scott, who was the Accessory Transit Company agent in Greytown between

1855 and 1857, swore under oath before the New York Supreme Court in April 1861 that all told about eleven thousand men traveled to Nicaragua on "emigrant tickets" and joined Walker's army.

The correct number probably lies somewhere between these two estimates, roughly five thousand in all, more or less. At least 50 percent of these recruits—Scott swore it was most of them—died in the course of the Nicaraguan bloodbath, including both of William Walker's brothers, Norvell and James. (Undoubtedly more Americans died fighting for Walker in Nicaragua during 1855–57 than died in battle in the Spanish-American War of 1898, when there were only 385 U. S. battle deaths.)

General Henningsen estimated the total Central American allied forces at 17,800, of whom at least 5,800 died of battle wounds; it is presumed that about 2,000 to 3,000 additional Central American servicemen died of disease—especially cholera.

APPROXIMATELY FIVE THOUSAND "VOLUNTEERS" FOUGHT, AT ONE TIME OR ANOTHER, IN WILLIAM WALKER'S ARMY IN NICARAGUA BETWEEN 1855 AND 1857: IT IS ESTIMATED THAT AT LEAST HALF DIED OF WOUNDS OR DISEASE

THE LATE GENERAL WALKER.

WE publish herewith, as matter of history, the portrait of the famous filibuster Walker, who was executed in Honduras on 12th ult. His life had been eventful and romantic.

He was only thirty-six years old when he died. Born at Nashville, Tennessee, in 1824, he was bred a lawyer: his father, a Scotch banker, occupied a prominent position in society, and enjoyed the respect of the community in which he lived. The son was a scape-grace. He failed as a lawyer; tried medicine, and achieved no particular success in that profession; finally fell back on the press, and so, in 1851, at the dawn of civilization on the Pacific slopes, he looms up as the editor of a paper at San Francisco.

It seems likely that the unsettled and turbulent temper of the people with whom he lived shaped the uncertain aspirations of William Walker. He had not been very long in California, and was doing a good business, when he suddenly crossed the frontier, and, squatting on some unoccupied land in Northern Mexico, proclaimed "an independent Republic of Lower California." This farce did not last long. There was a stir among the Mexican authorities, and an appearance of vigilance among the United States troops; but the point of the struggle was that the "independent Republic" and her newly-constituted rulers had nothing to eat. Walker surrendered himself and his party to a revenue officer of the United States, went through the form of a trial, and was promptly acquitted. At that day filibusterism was all the rage.

Not cured by experience, but rather encouraged by the sympathy his not very glorious exploits had won, Walker two years afterward undertook his second filibustering affray. The Democrats of Nicaragua offered him twenty thousand acres of land to fight on their side against the aristocratic party. A similar offer led Sir De Lacy Evans to fight against the Carlists in Spain, General Guyon to take a command in the Hungarian army of independence, Lord Cochrane to take a leading command in South America; Lafayette and Steuben fought for less in the United States, General Church was satisfied with less in Greece, Colonel Upton in Russia. General Walker made some further stipulations on behalf of his men, then chartered his vessel.

Five years ago last May that vessel, the *Vesta*, lay in the harbor of San Francisco, with General Walker and fifty-six men on board. She was under seizure. A deputy-sheriff's officer had possession. At midnight on Monday, the 4th May, Walker requested the sheriff's officer to step below to examine some documents in the cabin. The unsuspecting official complied. The door shut, he was informed that he was a prisoner.

"There, Sir," said Walker, in a slow, drawling voice, "are cigars and Champagne; and there are handcuffs and irons. Pray take your choice."

The deputy, a sensible man, took the former, and was in a very happy frame of mind when he was put on board the steam-tug to be taken back to the scene of his official duties. In the month of June General Walker arrived in Nicaragua. The Serviles were prepared in force to resist him; he fought a battle every three weeks. The capture of Granada was quickly followed by the massacre at Virgin Bay, and the necessary inauguration of General Walker's power in Nicaragua.

In the course of a short while a treaty of peace was signed between the contending forces; a native named Patricio Rivas was appointed President, and Walker General-in-chief of the army. This was the culminating moment of Walker's career. He held the real power in the Government of Nicaragua, Rivas being simply his tool. He had a fine transit route in full operation, which brought him hundreds of immigrants every month. Great Britain and the United States, sick of the unsuccessful endeavors of the Spanish Americans to establish stable governments, were both ready to recognize and support him. In this country especially every one was in his favor; he could have obtained money and men to any extent on a mere requisition. Finally, there is reason to believe that the best people in Nicaragua were fascinated by his brilliant success, and really believed that he was destined to be the regenerator of their country.

All this fair edifice of present power and future prospects Walker now proceeded deliberately to

THE LATE GENERAL WALKER, THE FILIBUSTER.

destroy. He shot Corral, his old foe, the head of the Serviles—a Central American gentleman of high standing—charging him with having plotted against the government they had combined together to establish. He revoked, without cause, the transit grant to the Nicaragua Company, and seized steamers belonging to American citizens, thus shutting himself and his new country out from the world, and closing the door to immigration. He made war upon Costa Rica, and managed matters so badly that his troops were beaten at the first encounter. He lost patience with Rivas, dismissed him, and usurped the Presidency. From that moment to the close of the Nicaraguan campaign his history was one of defeat, disaster, disappointment, and distress. The Nicaraguans and Costa Ricans combined against him; drove him from place to place, and at last so beleaguered him that, had it not been for the presence of an American sloop of war, which received him and his followers on board, he must have perished then and there. So ended the second filibustering expedition of Walker.

The third and fourth expeditions, both directed against Nicaragua, may be briefly disposed of. They were both ill-advised, and ill-planned; they both failed miserably; both would have terminated fatally for Walker and his followers but for the kindly interference of American and British vessels of war.

Walker's fifth and last filibustering raid was originally intended to be prosecuted against the famous Bay Islands which Great Britain is just ceding to Honduras. Several Anglo-Saxon residents of the islands had expressed unwillingness to be handed back to Honduras; Walker saw the opportunity of erecting a new independent empire. Unfortunately for him, Honduras foresaw his game, and requested Great Britain to delay the cession of the islands. Thus disappointed, Walker cruised

about in the Bay of Honduras for some weeks, literally seeking what he might devour, and finally, to his ruin, fell upon Truxillo. Forced to evacuate this place by the British war vessel *Icarus*, he was chased to bay by the Hondurenos; and refusing to claim either British or American protection, he died the death of a soldier at the hands of the Honduras authorities. The details of his execution will be found in the news columns.

Walker was undoubtedly a mischievous man, better out of the world than in it. He never displayed any constructive ability; his energies were wholly destructive. He was brave, persevering, and energetic; but he had little or no foresight, no compunctions of honor or conscience, and not a spark of human pity in his breast. His works, from first to last, have been injurious rather than beneficial to the world.

A FICTITIOUS FILIBUSTER

Some fifty years after William Walker's death a San Francisco news-paperman named H. C. Parkhurst decided to revive interest in Walker in order to stimulate newspaper circulation. During 1909–10, writing for the "San Francisco Chronicle" under the pseudonym "CLINTON ROLLINS," he vividly described Walker's invasions of Sonora and Nicaragua pretending to be a highly critical "eyewitness." Rollins in reality was a fake—a figment of Parkhurst's imagination who never existed.

[Factfinding: courtesy of
Dr. Alejandro Bolaños G., Masaya, Nicaragua.]

Walker's soldiers, although inevitably outnumbered by the enemy, were formidable fighters. About nine-tenths were American, mostly from the Atlantic states and California. They were a mixed breed, coming from all walks of life and ranging from a few wealthy college-educated aristocrats to some lowly ex-convicts. These rough-and-tumble adventurers had one thing in common—exceptional courage.

Many years later General Henningsen, who served as an officer in the Confederate army during the Civil War, testified concerning the extraordinary fortitude of Walker's filibusters in Nicaragua:

> I have often seen them marching with a broken or compound-fractured arm in splints, and using the other to fire the rifle or revolver. Those with a fractured thigh, or wounds which rendered them incapable of removal, often (or rather, in early times, always) shot themselves, sooner than fall into the hands of the enemy. Such men do not turn up in the average of every-day life, nor do I ever expect to see their like again. I was on the Confederate side in many of the bloodiest battles of the late war; but I aver that if, at the end of that war, I had been allowed to pick five thousand of the bravest Confederate or Federal soldiers I ever saw, and could resurrect and pit against them one thousand of such men as lie beneath the orange trees of Nicaragua, I feel certain that the thousand would have scattered and utterly routed the five thousand within an hour. All military science failed, on a suddenly given field, before assailants who came on at a run, to close with their revolvers, and who thought little of charging a battery, pistol in hand.

The world remembers successful men, but failures are soon forgotten. After the catastrophic holocaust of the Civil War, William Walker, the "gray-eyed man of destiny," having enjoyed a brief period of triumph and renown, gradually sank into oblivion.

But not everyone forgot. Joaquin Miller, a nineteenth-century frontier poet, idolized the Filibuster. Although he had not been with Walker in Nicaragua, he was so impressed by this quixotic soldier of fortune that he wrote a lengthy poem eulogizing his Byronic hero, entitled "With Walker in Nicaragua." Some years after Walker's death, Miller visited Truxillo, Honduras, to pay homage to the Filibuster's grave. The follow-

ing lines selected from Miller's "With Walker in Nicaragua"
commemorate that visit:

> He lies low in the levelled sand,
> Unsheltered from the tropic sun,
> And now of all he knew not one
> Will speak him fair in that far land.
> Perhaps 'twas this that made me seek,
> Disguised, his grave one winter-tide;
> A weakness for the weaker side,
> A siding with the helpless weak.
>
> Success had made him more than king;
> Defeat made him the vilest thing
> In name, contempt or hate can bring;
> So much the leaden dice of war
> Do make or mar of character.
>
> The Carib sea comes in so slow!
> It stays and stays, as loath to go,
> A sense of death is in the air,
> A sense of listless, dull despair,
> As if Truxillo, land and Tide,
> And all things, died when Walker died.

ILLUSTRATION ACKNOWLEDGMENTS

Courtesy of the Latin American Library, Tulane University: frontispiece and 75, 131, 147, 148, 164 . . . Courtesy of King Features Syndicate, Inc., 1941: vi . . . Ray Pike Studio, Nashville: viii, 203 left and right . . . Courtesy of Mrs. Charles P. Luckett: xii, 2 . . . Courtesy of University of Pennsylvania Archives: 3, 4 . . . Courtesy of the Leonard Huber Collection, Historic New Orleans Collection (from an oil painting by R. Riboni): 8 . . . Courtesy of Library of Congress: 15, 105, 140, 141, 146 . . . Courtesy of the Filson Club, Louisville: *Lopez's Expeditions to Cuba,* by Anderson C. Quisenberry, 1906: 17 . . . John Russell Bartlett. *Personal Narrative of Explorations and Incidents.* New York, 1854: 28, 51 . . . Courtesy of the California Historical Society, San Francisco: 31, 120 bottom, 145 right, 149, 183 . . . Courtesy of the Arizona Historical Society: 35 . . . Courtesy of the Huntington Library, San Marino, California: 38, 41, 43 top, 43 right (from *Pen Knife Sketches,* by Charles Nahl. Sacramento, 1853), 45 (from *National Magazine,* June 1854), 50, 66 bottom, 167 top (from *California Illustrated,* by J. M. Letts, 1852), 188 . . . T. Robinson Warren. *Dust and Foam.* New York: Charles Scribner, 1859: 39 . . . Courtesy of the Bettmann Archive: 43 bottom, 68 . . . Maps by William Streckfuss: endpapers and 53, 65, 73 . . . Courtesy of Federal Archives and Records Center, San Bruno, California: 56 . . . *Leslie's Illustrated Weekly,* 1879: 58 . . . Courtesy of the Historical Society of Pennsylvania: 61, 122, 190 . . . Courtesy of the Mariners' Museum, Newport News, Virginia: 63 . . . Courtesy of the Library Company of Philadelphia: 66 top . . . *Frank Leslie's Illustrated Newspaper,* 1855–57: 62, 80, 81, 85, 91, 93, 95, 96, 97, 98, 101, 103, 104, 116, 125, 127, 132, 135, 139, 159 top, 159, middle, 169, 179, 191 . . . William E. Simmons. *The Nicaragua Canal.* London: Harper & Brothers, 1900: 67 top . . . *San Francisco Pictorial Magazine.* May 30, 1857: 67 bottom, 216 . . . Courtesy of Dr. Alejandro Bolaños G.: 69 . . . Courtesy of the Bancroft Library: 70, 120 left, 159 bottom, 166 . . . Bedford Pim. *The Gate of the Pacific.* London: Lovell Reeve & Co., 1863: 77, 174 . . . *Harper's Weekly,* 1857–60: 79, 86, 117, 157, 158, 161, 172 bottom, 181, 212, 213 . . . E. G. Squier. *Nicaragua.* New York: Harper & Brothers, 1860: 82 . . . Courtesy of New York Public Library: 87 . . . Courtesy of Louisville Free Public Library: 108, 109, 110, 111, 128 left . . . Directory and Gazetteer. San Francisco, October 1856: 120 right . . . Courtesy of Archivo Nacional, San José, Costa Rica: 124, 175, 186, 187, 193 . . . Courtesy of Duke University, Perkins Library, Appleton Oaksmith Collection: 128 bottom, 130 . . . James Jeffrey Roche. *The Story of the Filibusters.* New York: T. Fisher Unwin, 1891: 129, 155 . . . Courtesy of Museo Nacional, San José, Costa Rica: 133 top . . . Courtesy of Henry M. Keith: 133 bottom . . . Guillermo Solano Noguera: 134 . . . After an old family portrait. Credit Francisco Vijil. *Datos Historicos.* Granada, Nicaragua, 1930: 137 . . . Courtesy of Tennessee Historical Society, State Library and Archives, Nashville. John P. Heiss scrapbook, ca. 1855–57: 145 left, 189 . . . Courtesy of Relaciones públicas del Ejército de Guatemala: 152 . . . Courtesy of the Museum of San Jacinto, Nicaragua: 153 left, 154 . . . Courtesy of Imprenta Hospicio, León, Nicaragua: 153 right . . . John D. Billings. *Hardtack and Coffee.* Boston: George M. Smith & Co., 1887: 163, 172 left top . . . A. G. Menocal. *Report of U.S.-Nicaragua Surveying Party.* Washington, D.C.: 1886: 167 bottom . . . Courtesy of New Orleans Public Library: 6, 171 . . . Courtesy of the *New York Times:* 176, 177 . . . Rebecca Paulding Meade. *Life of Hiram Paulding.* New York: The Baker & Taylor Co., 1910: 185 . . . The *Illustrated London News:* 198, 199 . . . James Carson Jamison. *With Walker in Nicaragua.* Columbia, Mo.: E. W. Stephens Publishing Company, 1909: 201 left and right . . . Archivo Nacional, Tegucigalpa, Honduras: 206, 207 . . . Courtesy of *La Prensa,* Managua, Nicaragua: dust jacket and 209 top . . . Courtesy of Adolfo Midence Soto, Tegucigalpa, Honduras: 209 bottom . . . Courtesy of *San Francisco Chronicle:* 214 . . .

Many illustrations in this book appeared originally in *Frank Leslie's Illustrated Newspaper* (later *Leslie's Illustrated Weekly*). Publication of this popular illustrated periodical commenced in New York in 1855 and continued until 1922.

Harper's Weekly, another prominent illustrated news magazine, was founded in New York in 1857 and discontinued in 1916.

BIBLIOGRAPHY

ABDULLAH, ACHMED and COMPTON, PARKEN-HAM T. *Dreamers of Empire*. New York: Frederick A. Stokes Company, 1929.

ADAMS, JAMES TRUSLOW. *America's Tragedy*. New York: C. Scribner's Sons, 1934.

ALLEN, MERRITT PARMALEE. *William Walker, Filibuster*. New York: Harper & Brothers, 1932.

Alta California (San Francisco), 1853–60.

ANDREWS, WAYNE. *The Vanderbilt Legend*. New York: Harcourt, Brace and Company, 1941.

Associated Press. *The Official Associated Press Almanac*. New York, 1973.

BANCROFT, HUBERT HOWE. *History of Central America*. Vol. 3. San Francisco: The History Company, 1887.

"BARD, SAMUEL A." (pseudonym of Ephraim George Squier). *Waikna; Or, Adventures on the Mosquito Shore* (a facsimile republication of the 1855 edition, with an introduction and index by Daniel E. Alleger). Gainesville: University of Florida Press, 1965.

BASS, J. M. "William Walker." *American Historical Magazine* 3, no. 3 (1898).

BELT, THOMAS. *The Naturalist in Nicaragua*. London: John Murray, 1874.

BRIDGES, C. A. "The Knights of the Golden Circle: A Filibustering Fantasy." *Southwestern Historical Quarterly* 44, no. 3 (January 1941).

CAIGER, STEPHEN L. *British Honduras, Past and Present*. London: George Allen & Unwin Ltd., 1951.

CALDERÓN RAMIREZ, SALVADOR. *Alrededor de Walker*. El Salvador: Ministerio de Instrucción Pública, 1929.

CALDWELL, ROBERT G. *The Lopez Expeditions to Cuba, 1848–1851*. Princeton: Princeton University Press, 1915.

CARR, ALBERT Z. *The World and William Walker*. New York: Harper & Row, 1963.

CLAPP, THEODORE. *Autobiographical Sketches*. Boston: Phillips, Sampson & Company, 1858.

CLARKE, JAMES MITCHELL. "Antonio Melendrez: Nemesis of William Walker in Baja California." *Quarterly of the California Historical Society* 12, no. 4 (December 1933).

CLELAND, ROBERT G. "Bandini's Account of William Walker's Invasion of Lower California." *Huntington Library Quarterly* (San Mateo, Calif.) 7 (1944).

CRAMER, FLOYD. *Our American Neighbor*. New York: Frederick A. Stokes Company, 1929.

CRENSHAW, OLLINGER. "The Knights of the Golden Circle." *American Historical Review* 47, no. 1 (October 1941).

CROFFUT, W. A. *The Vanderbilts and the Story of Their Fortune*. Chicago: Belford, Clarke & Company, 1886.

Crónicas y Comentarios. San José, Costa Rica: Imprenta Universal, 1956.

CROWE, FREDERICK. *The Gospel in Central America*. London: C. Gilpin, 1850.

CROWTHER, SAMUEL. *The Romance and Rise of the American Tropics*. Garden City, New York: Doubleday, Doran & Company, Inc., 1929.

Daily Crescent, The (New Orleans), 1848–50.

DARÍO, RUBÉN. *Poesía*. Libros Poeticos Completos. Mexico City: Fondo de Cultura Económica, 1952.

D'AUVERGNE, E. B. F. *Envoys Extraordinary*. London: George G. Harrap & Co. Ltd., 1937.

DAVIS, RICHARD HARDING. *Real Soldiers of Fortune*. New York: Charles Scribner's Sons, 1911.

DE BOW, J. D. B. "The South American States." *De Bow's Review* 6 (1848): 9.

De Bow's Review (Central America). July 1856, pp. 1–60.

Delta, The (New Orleans), 1853–60.

"Destiny of Nicaragua, The." *Blackwood's Magazine* 79 (1856): 314–16.

DEUTSCH, H. *William Walker Chronology.* New Orleans: Tulane University Press, 1933.

DOUBLEDAY, C. W. *Reminiscences of the "Filibuster" War in Nicaragua.* New York: G. P. Putnam's Sons, 1886.

DUFOUR, CHARLES L. *Gentle Tiger.* Baton Rouge: Louisiana State University Press, 1957.

Durham. Duke University, Perkins Library. Appleton Oaksmith papers and scrapbook (circa 1855–57).

DUVAL, MILES P., JR. *Cadiz to Cathay.* Palo Alto: Stanford University Press, 1940.

El Nicaraguense (Granada, Nicaragua), 1855–56.

"Experience of Samuel Absalom, Filibuster, The." *Atlantic Monthly,* December 1859 and January 1860.

FOLKMAN, DAVID I., JR. *The Nicaragua Route.* Salt Lake City: University of Utah Press, 1972.

FORBES, ROBERT H. *Crabb's Filibustering Expedition into Sonora, 1857.* Tucson: Arizona Silhouettes, 1952.

Frank Leslie's Illustrated Newspaper, 1855–60.

Gaceta de Guatemala, 1855.

GREENE, LAURENCE. *The Filibuster.* Indianapolis: The Bobbs-Merrill Company, 1937.

GUIER, ENRIQUE. *William Walker.* San José, Costa Rica, 1971.

Harper's Weekly, 1857–60.

HICKS, JIMMIE. "Some Letters concerning the Knights of the Golden Circle in Texas, 1860–1861." *Southwestern Historical Quarterly* 45, no. 1 (July 1961).

HITTELL, THEODORE H. *History of California.* San Francisco: N. J. Stone Company, 1898.

———. "Historical Account of Walker, the Filibuster" (unpublished manuscript). 1915. Sutro Library, California State Library, San Francisco.

HOYT, EDWIN P. *Commodore Vanderbilt.* Chicago: Reilly & Lee Co., 1962.

HUDSON, RANDALL O. "The Filibuster Minister: The Career of John Hill Wheeler as United States Minister to Nicaragua, 1854–1856." *North Carolina Historical Review* 49, no. 3 (July 1972).

HURTADO CHAMORRO, ALEJANDRO. *William Walker: Ideales y Propósitos.* Granada, Nicaragua, 1965.

Information Please Almanac. New York: Information Please, 1975.

JAMISON, JAMES CARSON. *With Walker in Nicaragua.* Columbia, Mo.: E. W. Stephens Publishing Company, 1909.

KARNES, THOMAS L. *The Failure of Union.* Chapel Hill: University of North Carolina Press, 1961.

KEASBEY, LINDLEY MILLER. *The Nicaragua Canal and the Monroe Doctrine.* New York: G. P. Putnam's Sons, 1896.

KEMBLE, JOHN H. *The Panama Route.* New York: Da Capo Press, 1972.

LANE, WHEATON J. *Commodore Vanderbilt.* New York: Alfred A. Knopf, 1942.

LEWIS, OSCAR. *Sea Routes to the Gold Fields.* New York: Alfred A. Knopf, 1949.

Louisville Times, 1856–60.

LUCAS, DANIEL B. *Nicaragua: War of the Filibusters.* Richmond: B. F. Johnson Publishing Company, 1896.

MACAULAY, NEILL. *The Sandino Affair.* Chicago: Quadrangle Books, 1967.

McGOWAN, EDWARD. *The Strange Eventful History of Parker H. French.* Los Angeles: Glen Dawson, 1958.

MANNING, WILLIAM R., ed. *Diplomatic Correspondence of the United States.* Vol. 4. Washington, D.C.: Carnegie Endowment for International Peace, 1934.

MAY, ROBERT E. *The Southern Dream of a Caribbean Empire.* Baton Rouge: Louisiana State University Press, 1973.

MEADE, REBECCA PAULDING. *Life of Hiram Paulding.* New York: The Baker & Taylor Company, 1910.

Merck Manual of Diagnosis and Therapy, The. Rahway, N. J.: Merck & Co., 1966.

MEYER, HARVEY K. *Historical Dictionary of Nicaragua.* Metuchen, N. J.: The Scarecrow Press, Inc., 1972.

Mobile Register, 1856–60.

MORISON, SAMUEL ELIOT. *The Oxford History of the American People.* New York: Oxford University Press, 1965.

MUNRO, DANA G. *The Five Republics of Central America.* New York: Oxford University Press, 1918.

Nashville. Tennessee Historical Society, State Library and Archives. John P. Heiss papers and scrapbook (circa 1855–57).

Nashville Daily Gazette, 1856–60.

Nashville Republican Banner, 1856–60.

Nashville Union and American, 1856–60.

NEUMANN, ALFRED. *Strange Conquest.* New York: Ballantine Books, 1954.

New Orleans. Tulane University, Latin American Library. Fayssoux Collection of William Walker papers.

New Orleans Bee, 1851.

New Orleans Courier, 1851.

New Orleans Picayune, 1856–60.

New Orleans Sunday Times, 1857.

New-York Daily Times, 1853–60.

New York Evening Post, 1856–60.

New York Herald, 1856–60.

New York Sun, 1856–60.

New York Tribune, 1856–60.

NORTH, ARTHUR WALBRIDGE. *Camp and Camino in Lower California.* New York: The Baker & Taylor Company, 1910.

OBREGÓN LORIA, RAFAEL. *La Campaña del Tránsito.* San José, Costa Rica: Editorial Universitaria, 1956.

OLIPHANT, LAURENCE. *Patriots and Filibusters.* London: William Blackwood and Sons, 1860.

PEREZ, JERONIMO. *Obras Históricas Completas.* Managua, Nicaragua: Imprenta y Encuadernación Nacional, 1928.

PERKINS, DEXTER. *The Monroe Doctrine, 1826–67.* Baltimore: Johns Hopkins University Press, 1933.

POWELL, E. ALEXANDER. *Gentlemen Rovers.* New York: Charles Scribner's Sons, 1913.

Putnam's Magazine, April 1857, pp. 425–35.

QUISENBERRY, ANDERSON C. *Lopez's Expeditions to Cuba 1850–1851.* Louisville: The Filson Club, 1906.

RATTERMAN, ELLEANORE. "With Walker in Nicaragua." *Tennessee Historical Magazine* 1 (1915).

RIPLEY, ELIZA M. *Social Life in Old New Orleans.* New Orleans: D. Appleton & Company, 1912.

RIPPY, J. FRED. "Anglo-American Filibusters and the Gadsden Treaty." *Hispanic American Historical Review* 5, no. 2 (May 1922).

ROCHE, JAMES JEFFREY. *The Story of the Filibusters.* New York: T. Fisher Unwin, 1891.

RODRIGUEZ, MARIO. *A Palmerstonian Diplomat in Central America.* Tucson: University of Arizona Press, 1964.

———. *Central America.* Englewood Cliffs, N. J.: Prentice-Hall, 1965.

RODRIGUEZ BETETA, VIRGILIO. *Transcendencia Nacional e Internacional de la Guerra de Centro America contra Walker y sus Filibusteros.* Guatemala City: Editorial del Ejército, 1960.

"ROLLINS, CLINTON" (pseudonym of H. C. Parkhurst.) "Filibustering with Walker." *San Francisco Chronicle,* 31 October 1909 to 6 February 1910.

San Diego Herald, 28 January 1854.

San Francisco Daily Herald, 1850–55.

SCROGGS, WILLIAM O. *Filibusters and Financiers.* New York: The Macmillan Company, 1916.

SHAW, FREDERICK T. *Dime American Comic Songster.* New York: Frederic A. Brady, 1859.

SHERMAN, STUART P. *The Poetical Works of Joaquin Miller.* New York: G. P. Putnam's Sons, 1923.

SHUCK, OSCAR T. *Historical Abstract of San Francisco.* Vol. 1. San Francisco, 1897.

SIMMONS, WILLIAM E. *The Nicaragua Canal.* London: Harper & Brothers, 1900.

SMITH, ARTHUR D. HOWDEN. *Commodore Vanderbilt: An Epic of American Achievement.* New York: Robert M. McBride & Company, 1927.

SOTO V., MARCO A. *Guerra Nacional de Centro-america*. Guatemala City: Editorial del Ministerio de Educación Publica, 1957.

SOULÉ, FRANK; GIHON, JOHN H.; and NISBET, JAMES. *Annals of San Francisco*. New York: D. Appleton & Company, 1855.

SQUIER, EPHRAIM GEORGE. *Nicaragua*. New York: Harper & Brothers, 1860.

STOUT, JOSEPH ALLEN, JR. *The Liberators*. Los Angeles: Westernlore Press, 1973.

STOUT, PETER F. *Nicaragua: Past, Present and Future*. Philadelphia: J. E. Potter, 1859.

THOMAS, JANE H. *Old Days in Nashville, Tennessee* (reprinted from the *Nashville Daily American*), 1897.

TRUMAN, BENJAMIN CUMMINGS. *The Field of Honor*. New York: Ford's Howard & Hulbert, 1884.

TWAIN, MARK. *Travels with Mr. Brown*. New York: Alfred A. Knopf, 1940.

URBAN, CHESTER STANLEY. "New Orleans and the Cuban Question during the Lopez Expeditions of 1849–1851." *Louisiana Historical Quarterly* 22, no. 4 (October 1939).

_____. "The Idea of Progress and Southern Imperialism: New Orleans and the Caribbean, 1845–1861." Ph.D. dissertation, Northwestern University, 1943.

VON HOLST, H. *The Constitutional and Political History of the United States*. Translated from the German by John J. Laylor. Chicago: Callaghan & Company, 1885.

WALKER, JAMES W. G. *Ocean to Ocean*. Chicago: A. C. McClurg & Co., 1902.

WALKER, WILLIAM. "Mexico and Central America." April 1858. Courtesy of Bancroft Library. University of California, Berkeley.

_____. "The Unity of Art." Address delivered before the Alumni Society of the University of Nashville, 3 October 1848.

_____. *The War in Nicaragua*. Mobile: S. H. Goetzel & Co., 1860.

WALLACE, EDWARD S. *Destiny and Glory*. New York: Coward-McCann, Inc., 1957.

WARREN, HARRIS G. *The Sword Was Their Passport*. Baton Rouge: Louisiana State University Press, 1943.

WARREN, T. ROBINSON. *Dust and Foam*. New York: Charles Scribner, 1859.

Washington, D.C. Library of Congress. Wheeler scrapbooks.

Washington, D.C. National Archives. Sworn deposition R-676. Costa Rican claims. Joseph N. Scott, New York Supreme Court. Re Accessory Transit Co. April 1861.

WEBSTER'S GEOGRAPHICAL DICTIONARY. Springfield, Mass.: G. & C. Merriam Company, 1962.

WEBSTER'S GUIDE TO AMERICAN HISTORY. Springfield, Mass.: G. & C. Merriam Company, 1971.

WEINBERG, ALBERT K. *Manifest Destiny*. Baltimore: Johns Hopkins Press, 1935.

WELLS, WILLIAM V. *Walker's Expedition to Nicaragua*. New York: Stringer and Townsend, 1856.

WILGUS, A. CURTIS. "Official Expression of Manifest Destiny Sentiment concerning Hispanic America, 1848–1871." *Louisiana Historical Quarterly* 15 (1932): 486–506.

WINDROW, JOHN EDWIN. *John Berrien Lindsley*. Chapel Hill: University of North Carolina Press, 1938.

WOODWARD, ARTHUR, ed. *The Republic of Lower California, 1853–1854*. Los Angeles: Dawson's Bookshop, 1966.

WYLLYS, RUFUS KAY. *The French in Sonora, 1850–1854*. Berkeley: University of California Press, 1932.

_____. "William Walker's Invasion of Sonora, 1854." *Arizona Historical Review* 6, no. 4 (October 1935).

INDEX

Nicaragua Route 1851-1857

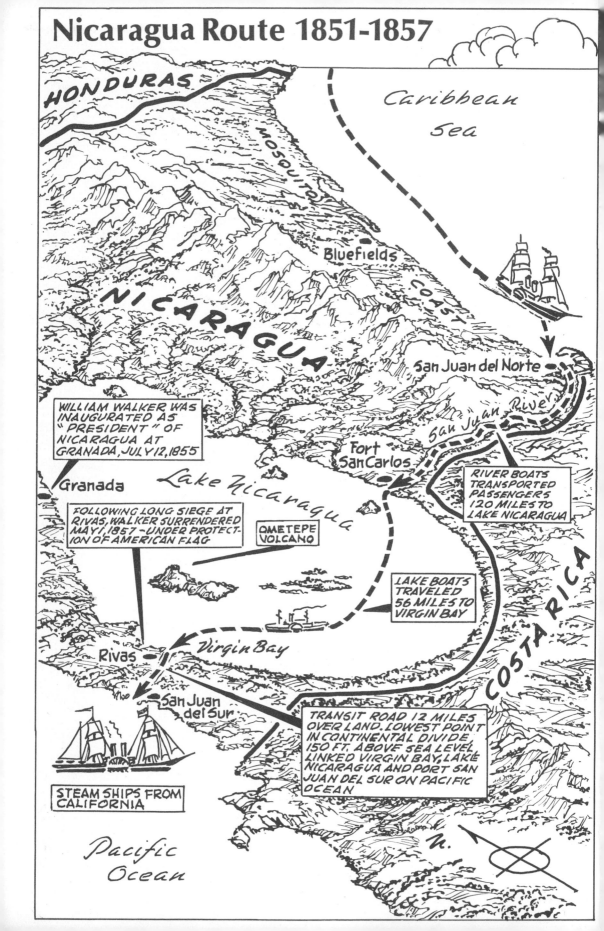

HONDURAS

Caribbean Sea

MOSQUITO COAST

Bluefields

NICARAGUA

San Juan del Norte

San Juan River

Fort San Carlos

WILLIAM WALKER WAS INAUGURATED AS "PRESIDENT" OF NICARAGUA AT GRANADA, JULY 12, 1855

Granada

Lake Nicaragua

RIVER BOATS TRANSPORTED PASSENGERS 120 MILES TO LAKE NICARAGUA

FOLLOWING LONG SIEGE AT RIVAS, WALKER SURRENDERED MAY 1, 1857 – UNDER PROTECTION OF AMERICAN FLAG

OMETEPE VOLCANO

LAKE BOATS TRAVELED 56 MILES TO VIRGIN BAY

COSTA RICA

Virgin Bay

Rivas

San Juan del Sur

TRANSIT ROAD 12 MILES OVER LAND. LOWEST POINT IN CONTINENTAL DIVIDE, 150 FT. ABOVE SEA LEVEL LINKED VIRGIN BAY, LAKE NICARAGUA AND PORT SAN JUAN DEL SUR ON PACIFIC OCEAN

STEAM SHIPS FROM CALIFORNIA

Pacific Ocean

N.